SNØHETTA

WHITE ARKITEKTER

OBSERVATORIUM

SPACE CRAFT²

MORE FLEETING ARCHITECTURE AND HIDEOUTS
EDITED BY ROBERT KLANTEN AND LUKAS FEIREISS

gesta1ten

CONTENT

CONTRIBUTORS

2012 ARCHITECTEN
2A+P ARCHITETTURA
70F ARCHITECTURE
A12
ACADEMY OF FINE ARTS MUNICH / INTERIOR DESIGN
ACCONCI STUDIO
ADAM KALKIN
AI WEIWEI
ALEKSANDER KONSTANTINOV
ALEXANDER BRODSKY
ALLAN WEXLER
AMENITY SPACE
ANARCHITECT LTD
ANDY HOLDEN
ANISH KAPOOR
ANNA GALTAROSSA & DANIEL GONZÁLEZ
ARCHEA ASSOCIATI
ATELIER BOW-WOW
ATELIER TEKUTO
ATMOS
BALL NOGUES STUDIO
BAUMRAUM
BELLEMO & CAT
BENJAMÍN MURÚA ARCHITECTS & CONSTANZA INFANTE S
BENJAMIN VERDONCK
BJÖRN DAHLEM
BORIS BERNASKONI
BRUT DELUXE
BUREAU DES MÉSARCHITECTURES
CARL-VIGGO HØLMEBAKK
CARLOS BUNGA
CARVE
CASEY BROWN ARCHITECTURE
CASTOR DESIGN
CHENG+SNYDER
CHIHARU SHIOTA
CHRIS BOSSE
CHRISTIAN POTTGIESSER / ARCHITECTURESPOSSIBLES
CHRISTOPH KLEMMT, HAJIME MURAMATSU, AND SVEN STEINER
  WITH SHIN EGASHIRA
CLAUS RICHTER
CONSTRUCTLAB
CONTAINERART
CORREIA RAGAZZI ARQUITECTOS
CUSTOMR
DADARA
DAN GRAHAM
DANA AND KARLA KARWAS
DANIELA BRAHM
DENIS OUDENDIJK & ROSA HAGEN
DESIGNSTUDIO
DIE BAUPILOTEN
DO-HO SUH
DORIS SALCEDO
DORTE MANDRUP ARKITEKTER
EAMON O'KANE
EBERHARD BOSSLET
ECOLOGICSTUDIO
EDOUARD SAUTAI
EIGHTYSEVEN
ELTONO & NURIA MORA
ERIK GÖNGRICH
ERIK OLOFSEN
ETIENNE BOULANGER
FANTASTIC NORWAY
FASHION ARCHITECTURE TASTE (FAT)
FELD72
FELIX JERUSALEM
FERNANDO AND HUMBERTO CAMPANA
FRANZ HÖFNER & HARRY SACHS
FRIENDS WITH YOU
FULGURO
GELITIN
GERDA STEINER & JÖRG LENZLINGER
GERMÁN DEL SOL
GIANNI BOTSFORD ARCHITECTS
GIUSEPPE GABELLONE

GO HASEGAWA & ASSOCIATES
GRAHAM HUDSON
GREGOR PASSENS
GREGOR SCHNEIDER
GUY BEN-NER
HAAS & HAHN
HACKENBROICH ARCHITEKTEN
HANS SCHABUS
HEATHERWICK STUDIO
HELEN & HARD
HELENA WILLEMEIT
HENRY KROKATSIS
HERBERT & MASON, KSUBI
HEW LOCKE
HOUSE IN THE CLOUDS
HUSOS
HÜTTEN & PALÄSTE / G.D.HOLZFREUNDE B.R.
I-BEAM DESIGN
ID-LAB
INTERBREEDING FIELD
ISAY WEINFELD
JASON RHOADES
JAVIER SENOSIAIN
JOE COLEMAN
JOHN KÖRMELING
JOLIAN & LUFT
JONAS LIVERÖD
JONAS WAGELL DESIGN & ARCHITECTURE
JOOST AKKERMANS
JUN AOKI & ASSOCIATES
JÜRGEN HEINERT, MICHAEL SAILSTORFER
KAI SCHIEMENZ
KALHÖFER-KORSCHILDGEN
KASBAH-HÄUSER
KEES VAN DER HOEVEN
KENNY SCHACHTER / ROVE & ZAHA HADID ARCHITECTS
KEVIN VAN BRAAK
KÖBBERLING KALTWASSER
KREISSL KERBER
KRIJN DE KONING
KRISTIN POSEHN
KUMIKO INUI
LAGOMBRA
LAND ARQUITECTOS
LARS Ø RAMBERG
LAVA / LABORATORY FOR VISONARY ARCHITECTURE ASIA PACIFIC
LES FRÈRES CHAPUISAT
LIZA LOU
LOS CARPINTEROS
LOY BOWLIN
LUCAS LENGLET
MARCEL SCHMALGEMEIJER
MARCIO KOGAN
MARJETICA POTRČ
MASS STUDIES
MATTONOFFICE
MAURER UNITED ARCHITECTS [MUA]
MICHAEL BEUTLER
MICHAEL ELMGREEN & INGAR DRAGSET
MICHAEL SAILSTORFER, JÜRGEN HEINERT
MICHEL DE BROIN
MISS ROCKAWAY ARMADA
MODULORBEAT – AMBITIOUS URBANISTS & PLANNERS
N55, ARTIST GROUP
NABA DESIGN SCHOOL
NATHAN COLEY
NENDO
NOX
O2 TREEEHOUSE
OBSERVATORIUM
OLAFUR ELIASSON
OLIVER BISHOP-YOUNG
ONIX
OSA OFFICE FOR SUBVERSIVE ARCHITECTURE
OSKAR LEO KAUFMANN
PATRICK DOUGHERTY
PETER CALLESEN

PEZO VON ELLRICHSHAUSEN
PHOEBE WASHBURN
PHOOEY ARCHITECTS
PIERRE MORENCY ARCHITECTE
PIET HEIN EEK
PJOTR MÜLLER
PRIMITIVO SUAREZ-WOLFE, GINGER WOLFE-SUAREZ
  AND MOIRA ROTH
PROJECT OR
RACHEL WHITEREAD
RAUMLABORBERLIN
RB ARKITEKTUR
REBAR
REFUNC.NL
RICHARD WILSON
RICHARD WOODS
RINTALA EGGERTSSON ARCHITECTS
ROBBIE ROWLANDS
ROB VOERMAN
ROCIO ROMERO
RODERICK ROMERO
ROSS STEVENS
ROTOR
RYUMEI FUJIKI+FUJIKI STUDIO, KOU::ARC
SABINE GROSS
SALZIG DESIGN
SAMI RINTALA
SANEI HOPKINS ARCHIETCTS
SCHOOL OF ARCHITECTURE, UNIVERSIDAD DE TALCA, CHILE
SCULP(IT) ARCHITECTEN
SEAN GODSELL ARCHITECTS
SEBASTIAN DENZ
SIMPARCH
SITU STUDIO
SKENE CATLING DE LA PENA
SNØHETTA
SOU FOUJIMOTO ARCHITECTS
SSD
STEPHAN KÖPERL, SYLVIA WINKLER, MARWA ZAKARIA
STORTPLAATS VAN DROMEN
STUDIO JAN HABRAKEN & ALISSIA MELKA TEICHROEW
STUDIO LUKASZ KOS
STUDIOMAMA
STUDIO ORTA
SUMER EREK
SUPERBLUE DESIGN
TAYLOR SMYTH ARCHITECTS
TERUNOBU FUJIMORI
THEATER HET AMSTERDAMSE BOS
THE FINCHMOB, REBAR & CMG LANDSCAPE
THE NEXT ENTERPRISE – ARCHITECTS
THOMAS BRATZKE
THOMAS RENTMEISTER
TILL GERHARD
TILMAN WENDLAND
TJEP.
TOBIAS PUTRIH
TOBIAS REHBERGER
TOKUJIN YOSHIOKA
TOMMIE WILHELMSEN
TOM SACHS
TOPOTEK 1
TRACEY EMIN
TREEHOUSE CREATIONS
TREEHOUSE WORKSHOP
TUMBLEWEED TINY HOUSE COMPANY
ULLMAYER SYLVESTER
UNFOLD
UNIVERSITY OF KASSEL
UNIVERSITY OF SHEFFIELD SCHOOL OF ARCHITECTURE
VIA GRAFIK
WHAT IF: PROJECTS
WHITE ARKITEKTER
WINTER / HÖRBELT
WORK ARCHITECTURE COMPANY
YAYOI KUSAMA
ZECC ARCHITECTEN

SPACE CRAFT2

MORE FLEETING ARCHITECTURE AND HIDEOUTS

LUKAS FEIREISS

THE NEXT EPISODE

Taking the discussion of space and building beyond the confines of academic preconceptions and university curricula is what distinguished the first Spacecraft book from the crowd. Spacecraft 2 follows in the footsteps of its popular predecessor, serving architects, artists, designers, and general readers alike as a valuable reference on the myriad techniques and practices to be found in the realm of fleeting architecture and hideouts.

To create this compendium, I have once again grazed the globe with open eyes, ears, and mind in search of new and inspiring projects that articulate novel ways of discovering and negotiating the creative potential of spatial design. The works presented in this volume expand our understanding of ephem-

eral architecture, unhinging conventional readings of the built environment. Above all, it is these moments of surprise – the unexpected encounters that capture and enchant us – that I will strive to communicate in the following pages.

BETWEEN STICKS AND STONES

The projects showcased in this volume are both ephemeral and dynamic, ranging from pavilions, art projects, and exhibition spaces to country houses, mobile habitats, and pop-up buildings. The opening chapter, Living in a Box, focuses on projects that literally return to square one in their obsession with cubic and often modular building units, such as cargo containers, but then take off on an adventurous exploration of rectangular superstructures and their creative possibilities.

This game with basic design principles is traced further in the second chapter. Let's Play House introduces the reader to numerous formalistic variations on the elementary form of a house. Four plain walls and a pitched roof – reminiscent in their simplicity of a child's drawing – become the subject here of various humorous transformations.

For some time now, all lights have switched to green. A new global awareness of our natural environment's vulnerability is setting the stage for active change. The third chapter, When Nature Calls, presents a variety of projects that respond to nature's plea for sustainability in a variety of fitting as well as ironic ways.

Walk This Way explores transit spaces such as passages, stairs, bridges, and mobile units of every shape and size. These architectural pathways seem to adapt fluidly to any given restraint within the built environment. By allowing us to experience architecture less as an object and more as a process, the projects showcased in this chapter dissolve physical constraints and question the very concept of built-up space.

The projects in the fourth chapter, Just Lose It, illustrate both the possibilities opened up by a loss of control or the breakdown of form in ever-eclectic constructions, and the potential of recycling waste materials for building construction. Everything from doors, windows, tyres, and cars to cardboard buildings and miniature cities made of salvaged goods can be found here.

Maintaining this accelerated pace, the final chapter, Blow Up, culminates in a firework of seemingly paradox architectural and artistic ventures that magnify the abandonment of customary approaches to built space. The title alone indicates the complexity of practices. With its intentional double meaning, Blow Up creates a bridge between spatially expanding, inflatable structures, on the one hand, and shuttered and ruptured constructions, on the other.

SPACED OUT

Spacecraft 2 is a vivid demonstration of how creative minds from all fields are crafting spaces that reflect the exchange, communication, and development entailed in contemporary building practices. This heterogeneous survey brings together an unusual collection of projects by young and, as yet, little-known talents, as well as by internationally renowned artists and architects, revealing a panoply of new and eclectic

working methods that transform and redefine existing conceptions of space and, even more importantly, intellectual structures beyond building.

I would like to express my sincere gratitude to all contributing artists, whose ingenious work has made this publication possible. In particular, I would like to thank the family and friends of French artist Etienne Boulanger, who tragically passed away while this book was still in progress.

What more can I say in conclusion than to honour the moment and make the best out of what we've got? If you enjoyed the first Spacecraft ride, you surely do not want to miss our second journey. So leave everything behind and come witness a new era of space exploration!

Lukas Feireiss is a curator, writer, and artist deeply involved in the discussion and mediation of architecture, art, and media beyond their disciplinary boundaries. He teaches at various universities worldwide.

CHAPTER 01

LIVING IN A BOX

SAMI RINTALA

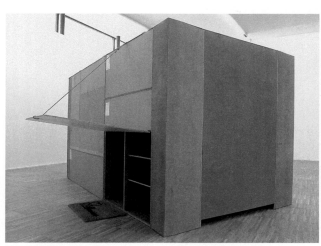

FRANZ HÖFNER & HARRY SACHS

SCHOOL OF ARCHITECTURE, UNIVERSIDAD DE TALCA, CHILE

The opening chapter, Living in a Box, focuses on a back-to-basics approach within architecture by referencing one of mankind's most mythical structures – the ark. The very concept of the ark, which derives from the Latin arca, meaning a box or chest for valuables, reveals a radical principle of space that serves as a prototype for basic, stand-alone, and context-free shelter and protection.

The myriad buildings presented in this chapter offer a surprising array of variations, ranging from cubic and somewhat modular building units to virtuoso explorations of rectangular superstructures. Castor Design's Sauna Box, for example, turns a conventional shipping container into a self-contained, traditional sauna with solar power and a wood-fired stove. The Phooey Architects use cargo containers to create an entire playground and activity centre for children, whereas the Amsterdam Bos Theater designs a breathtaking stage by placing containers and trailers on top of one another in seemingly random fashion. Pjotr Müller's House for Dr. Jung and Sami Rintala's Element House are yet further examples of boxes that appear to be randomly stacked, and they find their ultimate culmination in Rachel Whitread's famous House installation – a concrete cast of the inside of an entire Victorian terraced house, exhibited at the site of the original building.

On thing becomes clear: simple building modules can provide the raw material for structures that can be infinitely mobilised, manipulated, and transformed.

SNØHETTA
KIVIK ART CENTRE – PERCEPTUAL DISPLACEMENTS
Kivik, Sweden

'Kivik Start' is a series exploring the spatial and temporal relationships between photography, architecture, and landscape. It is the first phase in the establishment of a new contemporary art centre in Kivik, Sweden.

The solid concrete boxes attempt to capture the ghost of the timeless photographic image in the here-and-now of the construction. The site on Sweden's southeast coast is a mix of cleared pastures, wooded glades, rolling hills, and steep drop-offs. The strategic placement of the five concrete interventions invites the visitor to explore four discrete landscapes.

SCHOOL OF ARCHITECTURE, UNIVERSIDAD DE TALCA, CHILE
Rodrigo Sheward Giordano
PINOHUACHO OBSERVATION DECK
Pinohuacho, Villarica, Chile

The School of Architecture at the Universidad de Talca in Chile brings architecture to places where there is none. Young architects are asked to manage, design, and build spaces that foster dialogue in Chile's remote countryside. This project is located a one-hour walk up a winding track that climbs the slopes of a hill to its summit and consists of two volumes situated eighty metres apart. The first one looks onto the side of the Villarrica volcano, while the other faces the lakes Calafquén and Panguipulli. The main body is a storage facility that is used as a lair for the hunters of wild boar in the winter. During the summer, it is a stopover for hikers, naturalists, and the curious.

CORREIA RAGAZZI ARQUITECTOS
CASA NO GERÊS

Caniçada, Vieira do Minho, Gerês,
Portugal

The Casa No Gerês both reconstructs and augments a ruin into a weekend retreat on a plot with extraordinary morphological characteristics. The plot is located in a protected natural area and has a concrete construction to protect against all weather conditions.

The architect's design is a dramatic one: a concrete bar that cantilevers for about a third of its length. This decision helps to minimise the footprint of the house while reaching out towards the water and inserting the occupants into the setting. The cantilevered tip houses the dining area, kitchen, living room, and entrance in the midsection and the bedrooms in the rear – a fairly straightforward plan for an otherwise daring design.

SEAN GODSELL ARCHITECTS
ST ANDREW'S BEACH HOUSE
Victoria, Australia

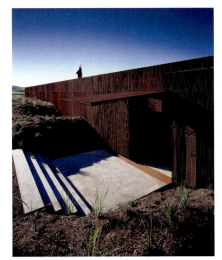

page 12
SEAN GODSELL ARCHITECTS
ST ANDREW'S BEACH HOUSE
Victoria, Australia

St Andrew's Beach on Victoria's Mornington Peninsula is unusual in that it is one of the few locations in Australia where construction is permitted right on the foreshore. Normally, the coastline is protected as government-owned land. The site of this project is elevated and exposed to magnificent ocean views and, in the winter, to gale-force winds. The house has a protective outer skin made of oxidised steel industrial floor grating, which hinges open to form brise soleil shutters. The building is raised on columns, with parking and storage underneath.

page 13
SEAN GODSELL ARCHITECTS
GLENBURN HOUSE
Victoria, Australia

The site is twenty hectares of re-invigorated farmland with a national forest abutting the north boundary. The house is located at the top of a hill and enjoys panoramic views of quintessential Australian landscape. It is partially embedded in the hilltop as a means of protecting the occupants from the prevailing weather and buffering the west side of the building from extreme heat in summer.

MODULORBEAT – AMBITIOUS URBANISTS & PLANNERS
SWITCH +, A GOLDEN PAVILION FOR SCULPTURE PROJECTS MUENSTER 07
Münster, Germany

This temporary construction project was created to mark the occasion of the internationally renowned outdoor exhibition Skulptur Projekte Münster 07. Planned and supervised by Münster firm modularbeat, a twelve-metre-high parallelepiped, clad on all sides with the new copper alloy Gold, was built adjacent to the Museum of Art and Cultural History and the exhibition project office on a previously unused open square.

1

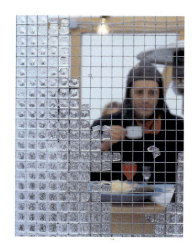

ARCHEA ASSOCIATI
NEMBRO LIBRARY
Nembro, Italy

For a library in this small town near Bergamo, Italy, Archea Associati were comissioned to incorporate a late-nineteenth-century C-shaped building into the original design. The extension is situated in front of the opening of the C-shape, forming an open court with the old building. A transparent glass volume is surrounded by a façade of red glazed earthenware tiles held in place by a frame of steel profiles, a construction method that enables the tiles to rotate and thus act as a sunscreen for the glazed inner façades. The result is a distinctive screen wall in which closed and open planes alternate in a continuous pattern created by the rotating ceramic elements.

page 14 / 1
ALEXANDER BRODSKY
ICE BAR
Klyazminskoye reservoir, Russia

In 2003 Russian artist Alexander Brodsky constructed an ice-crusted metal cage on a frozen lake – a glowing bar until the spring thaw.

ZECC ARCHITECTEN
HOUSE IN VRIEZENVEEN
Vriezenveen, Netherlands

This remarkable residential property is a prime example of how the Dutch landscape is being transformed. Historic farmhouses are making way for new, artificial abstract dwellings. The land itself is increasingly being used for recreational purposes rather than for agriculture. The dark silhouettes of the historic farmhouses provided the most important source of inspiration for this statuesque house in Vriezenveen.

The house is lengthened by an upper floor consisting of two separate elements that are offset towards the front and rear of the building. This produces a silhouette of apparently separate sections that stands out in the surrounding area. In addition, the formation of the upper floor creates a covered terrace at the rear and a carport at the front – elements that had been requested in the project brief.

1 | PIERRE MORENCY ARCHITECTE
CHALET DU CHEMIN BROCHU
Beaulac, Québec, Canada

A very personal project by Pierre Morency. The idea for the Chalet du Chemin Brochu was first planted in his mind by his children. One wanted a spaceship, but the other wanted a tree house. In the end, both got what they wanted. The family began by assembling three black cargo containers in a vacant lot in Montreal, wiring them, and then transporting them out to Brochu – a tiny village of about 800 inhabitants.

Rather than felling every tree in sight to expand the horizon and reduce dampness near the house, Morency opted to leave the trees where they were and to enjoy a rather different sort of view. Morency placed all three containers in such a way as to create the illusion that they could still move, when indeed they had been secured quite firmly. The top black box floats in space, away from its base: the spaceship.

2 | LAND ARQUITECTOS
SPA LAS PALMAS DE LEYDA
Las Palmas, Chile

The Spa by Land Arquitectos is an open space that feels protected on the exterior but allows an uninterrupted view from the inside. The passing of the hours during the day transforms the inside space. The outside skin made of wooden slats provides a degree of privacy.

KASBAH–HÄUSER
University of Art & Design Helsinki
& Kunsthochschule Kassel
HOUSE LIANE
Kassel, Germany

House Liane of the KasBaH Häuser
project. It is one of the five temporary guesthouses built for docu-
menta12 in Kassel. It is based on
a simple cubic form that shifts in
ever-complex configurations. The
roof light generated in this manner
brightens the space and opens it up
towards the sky.

KASBAH–HÄUSER
University of Art & Design Helsinki
& Kunsthochschule Kassel
THROUGH THE WALL
Kassel, Germany

Parallel to the conception of House
Liane, a number of slideable furniture pieces were designed that
create a connection between inner
and outer space.

page 19
PJOTR MÜLLER
HOUSE FOR DR. JUNG
Kröller-Müller Museum, Otterlo,
the Netherlands

On the terrain of the Kröller-Müller
Museum, Pjotr Müller designed a
building made of scrap wood. The
idea for the house arose from reading a book by Carl Gustav Jung in
which the psychoanalyst recalls
a dream about a house that could
be entered only at the top floor.
Running from the back to the front,
from the attic to the cellar, he found
a mythological sculpture in each
room. Müller deviates from this
dream by placing his own dream-
based figurines inside instead. The
building now consists of three almost
randomly stacked rectangular boxes.

SAMI RINTALA
ELEMENT HOUSE
Anyang, South Korea

The Element House by Sami Rintala is situated in the Anyang Public Art Park in the Seoul metropolitan area in South Korea. The building is standing on top of a small forest hill, along an outdoor route leading to the mountains in the far end of the park.

The main space is a large steel cube. Four smaller wooden rooms are connected to this space on different levels. In each of these small rooms, there is the presence of one element of nature: water in the cellar, soil in the courtyard, fire on the first floor, and air in the attic.

RINTALA EGGERTSSON ARCHITECTS
BOXHOME
Kåfjord, Norway

The prototypical Boxhome is a low-cost green dwelling. The project focuses on the quality of space, material, and natural light, and tries to reduce unnecessary floor area. Boxhome is a nineteen-square-metre dwelling with four rooms covering the basic living functions: a kitchen, bathroom, living rooms and bedroom.

CASEY BROWN ARCHITECTURE
PERMANENT CAMPING
Mudgee, Australia

Located on a remote, pristine mountain at a sheep station, this building is conceived as a retreat for one or two people. The structure is a two-storey, copper-clad tower; the sides open up on the ground level to provide wide verandas to the north, east, and west. The interior provides a sleeping loft and small kitchen.

KALHÖFER–KORSCHILDGEN
RAUM AUF ZEIT
Bonn, Germany

ONIX
KIOSK DOMIES TOEN
Pieterburen, Netherlands

This kiosk forms the entrance to the
Domies Toen Botanical Gardens in
Pieterburen and accommodates a
seating area and showcase.

1 | **FRANZ HÖFNER & HARRY SACHS**
HEIMKINO

Galerie Maerz, Linz, Austria

Two shelf systems are pushed together, creating a minimalist living room on the inside.

2 | **UNFOLD**
NOCTOUR BAR

Mechelen / Hof van Busleyden, Belgium

In the summer of 2006, four outside projections appeared in two remarkable venues in Mechelen. In the garden of the Hof van Busleyden, Unfold set up a summer bar. In the evening, during opening hours, the bar had an unusual shape. In the daytime, when the exhibition was closed but the garden still accessible, the bar was folded up into the shape of a simple, rectangular wooden box, as if it had fallen out of a gigantic set of blocks.

TJEP.
ROC CARE
Apeldoorn, Netherlands

This box is part of a reception area created by Dutch designers Tjep for the ROC professional training school in Apeldoorn. The idea of care has been visualised in different interior elements, such as this protective shelter and relaxation area, which is in the shape of a large box.

THOMAS RENTMEISTER
GEMÜTLICHKEITSHÜTTE (HUT OF COSINESS)
Museum Boijmans van Beuningen, Rotterdam, Netherlands

Thomas Rentmeister produces sculptures or, to be more precise, three-dimensional works that are cast from a plaster model according to the traditional process, but consist of polyester mixed with coloured pigments. This technique means that Rentmeister transforms the opaque, heavy plaster form into a thin-skinned, coloured polyester form, the surface of which is then polished to create a shiny, reflective sculpture.

CASTOR DESIGN
BETON BRUT
Toronto, Canada

For the Toronto Interior Design Show, Canadian Castor Design created Beton Brut, a concrete fishing hut with a wood stove, stools, bulb chandelier, and stools loaded with Christian imagery. The hut was an environment to showcase a new chandelier made from burnt-out light bulbs and the blind stool.

PRIMITIVO SUAREZ-WOLFE, GINGER WOLFE-SUAREZ AND MOIRA ROTH
SHELTER FOR POETRY
Yerba Buena Center for the Arts, San Francisco, USA

The Shelter for Poetry explores ideas of violence and protection through images, text, and built environment. It was based primarily on a poem entitled 'Bombs Provide the Only Light' by art historian and poet Moira Roth, who collaborated with the two artists on various aspects of the project. Shelter for Poetry is both a bomb shelter and a place for reading. Using concrete, mirror, and paper alongside light and darkness as media, the artists play with the contradictions of our physical and social framework. The project was conceptualised to evoke an intimate and collective viewing experience that explores reading and writing as a kind of action.

1 | **KENNY SCHACHTER / ROVE &**
ZAHA HADID ARCHITECTS
KENNY SCHACHTER / ROVE PAVILION
Art Basel, Miami, USA

Kenny Schachter ROVE and Zaha
Hadid Architects showcased this
stand-alone pavilion at Art Basel
Miami Beach.

2 | **MARCIO KOGAN**
VOLUME B
São Paulo, Brazil

Volume B, designed by Marcìo Kogan,
is the retail furniture store for
Vitra, located in São Paulo, Brazil.
The architect used the materials in
their extreme condition, such as visible concrete executed without any
concern to precision or finishing, or
the skin of the back volume, where
Kogan used various layers of a steel
frame that is normally employed
on the inside of concrete slabs and
which were found at the site.

page 29
OSKAR LEO KAUFMANN &
ALBERT RÜF
SYSTEM3
MoMA, New York, USA

The System3 home was developed
as an innovative building system
for future demands – especially
concerning mobility, flexibility, and
sustainability. The system is based
on the separation of a building into
'serving space' and 'naked space'.
The serving space is a completely
prefabricated serving unit that provides all staircases, kitchens, baths,
installations, electricity, and heating
and cooling systems for the entire
building. The naked space (space
that is defined only by the furniture
placed in it, such as a living room
or bedrooms) is formed by naked
elements: solid slabs of wooden
window skins. All naked elements are
also prefabricated and are delivered
directly from the factory to the
building site, where everything can
be assembled in a few days.

OSKAR LEO KAUFMANN &
ALBERT RÜF
SYSTEM3
MoMA, New York, USA

ROCIO ROMERO

1 | **MATTHEW AND ALLISON'S LVL**
New York, USA

2 | **ROCIO AND CALE'S LV**
Missouri, USA

The LV Home Series by Rocio Romero consists of modern kit homes that are affordable, easily built, and highly customisable. The architect provides the client with parts that make up the exterior shell of the LV home and can be delivered anywhere in the United States. By employing traditional construction materials and techniques, any general contractor can build the LV Home.

NENDO
BOOK HOUSE
Tokyo, Japan

By using bookshelves to clad the exterior walls, this combination of house and library protects the privacy of its inhabitants' living space while inviting visitors into the surrounding library. Semi-transparent FRP divides the interior and exterior spaces, allowing soft light to filter in between the bookshelves during the day, and letting the light leak out at night. Light creates a connection between inside and outside.

DAN GRAHAM
PAVILION
Johnen Galerie Berlin, Germany

Two-way mirror and stainless-steel
construction

LUCAS LENGLET
MOBILE STUDIO
Central Tax Office, Apeldoorn,
Netherlands

The Mobile Studio was designed on
commission by the Chief Government
Architect's Office and Sandberg
Institute as a semi-permanent artist's
residency to be used by artists and
designers. It was placed as a temporary art project on the grounds of the
Central Tax Office in Apeldoorn. The
aim was to design a mobile observation unit that could merge into its
surroundings. The unit is made for
one person to live and work in for a
limited stay.

1 | SAMI RINTALA
HOTEL KIRKENES
Kirkenes, Norway

The town of Kirkenes in northern Norway lies at the intersection of many cultures; here, the Sami, Russians, Norwegians, and Finns (that is, the Kvens) have long interacted with one another. As the result of an invitation to create a work of art in the centre of town, Sami Rintala constructed this hotel as a place for the seamen, fishermen, hunters, hikers, and fortune seekers passing through for the night.

The project was constructed in ten days on a small budget. It is an entirely wooden structure standing on a lightweight brick foundation. The whole interior is painted natural white for maximum light conditions during the winter, and exterior is brown-black to receive the sun's warmth and imitate the colour of the rocky seashore. The house is anchored to the pier rocks to match the rough weather conditions prevailing at the site. A large letter H is painted on the wall facing the city to facilitate the recognition of a hotel in the landscape of warehouses and containers.

2 | FRANZ HÖFNER & HARRY SACHS
INTERIOR
Galerie faux-mouvement, Metz, France

White exhibition walls were installed in the gallery by the artist duo Franz Höfner and Harry Sachs, creating a hidden apartment accessible to the public.

ETIENNE BOULANGER
SINGLE ROOM HOTEL
Skulpturenpark, Berlin, Germany

Single Room Hotel is an independent
space of thirty-two square metres
in size, located on a large undefined
area right in the centre of Berlin.
The habitable module, with electricity
and running water, is set up according to the standards of a two-star
hotel room. Hidden in its urban
setting, this hotel's specific nature
lies in its creation and production
process. The advertisements on its
exterior, an activating element of
involvement, allow the artist to create camouflage strategies applied
to the habitat while developing the
economic potential necessary for
supporting the project. By renting
and occupying this room for one or
more nights, the visitor activates the
work while fully enjoying its facilities.

STUDIO LUKASZ KOS
4TREEHOUSE
Lake Muskoka, Canada

Four trees in a forest were wrapped in a lattice-like skin, creating an intimate relationship between the natural setting and the architecture. The skin acts as a tree canopy, filtering sunlight in the interior spaces.

DESIGNSTUDIO
Mark Meyer
SEXYSHACK
Austin, Texas, USA

The sexySHACK is an exercise in materiality and standard stick-built framing. The building claims the entire area of the slab on which it stands, the stud walls cantilevering over the slab's edge. Atop the cellular polycarbonate sheathed walls sits a flat roof, whose cornice mimics the cantilevered walls below.

TAYLOR SMYTH ARCHITECTS
SUNSET CABIN
Lake Simcoe, Ontario, Canada

This cabin serves as a private retreat from the main cottage further up the hill, enhancing the client's enjoyment of the surrounding landscape in a location previously used to watch the sunset. The fully insulated glass cabin is encased on three sides by cedar slats. A green roof is planted with sedums and herbs to camouflage views of the cabin from the main cottage. The minimal furnishing includes a bed with built-in drawers, a wall of storage cabinets, and a wood-burning stove. The changes of both season and time of day continuously transform the cabin's presence and dynamics with the landscape.

page 36
DORTE MANDRUP ARKITEKTER
NEIGHBOURHOOD CENTRE
Copenhagen, Denmark

The renovation and expansion of the
Neighbourhood Centre was part of a
larger neighbourhood renewal plan.
The main objective was to connect
the building's many different activities
and, at the same time, ensure an
openness and accessibility for the
public. This additional building was
conceived as a 'children's tree house'
on trunks of oblique concrete columns. It houses a double-high hall and
lies as a freestanding glass-walled
structure, slightly turned between
the two tall neighbouring buildings,
which are covered with different
kinds of ivy. The supporting structure
in the hall consists of an exposed
framework of plywood covered with
thermal glazing panels in pine frames.

ROTOR
RDF181
Brussels, Belgium

The temporary head office and exhibition space of the Brussels-based
Rotor non-profit organisation hangs
against the blank sidewall of a town-
house. Built among four concrete
buttresses, which prop up the blank
wall, this construction is composed
entirely of industrial waste and
reusable materials. The site is a
piece of wasteland where a property
developer plans to build new homes,
and which was lent for a year while
waiting for planning permission. The
ground floor had to be kept free as a
parking space for the owner, which
is why the office, starting halfway
up the concrete buttresses, now
protrudes above the wall around the
site. Rotor defines this solution as
legal squatting.

THEATER HET AMSTERDAMSE BOS
Catharina Scholten
STAGE DESIGN FOR IVANOV PLAY
Amsterdam, Netherlands

This stage design by Catharina
Scholten was conceived for Anton
Chekhov's play "Ivanov" directed by
Jeroen van den Berg in an open-air
theatre close to Amsterdam. The
tumbledown structure is composed
of shipping containers and caravans
interconnected by a network of metal
stairways and gantries.

SCULP(IT) ARCHITECTEN
PRIVATE HOUSE
Antwerp, Belgium

This narrow house designed and built
by Sculp(it) Architecten serves as the
architect's private house and office.
Around sixty square metres to live
and work are divided over four floors.

HELEN & HARD
B-CAMP
Stavanger, Norway

Helen & Hard has worked on several recycling projects that reuse structures discarded by the oil industry. As such, this project utilises former industrial-site dwelling units as its building blocks. B-Camp is a low-budget dwelling alternative for young adults who like a short commute: a creative environment with adjoining recreational facilities and adjacent to the H&H studio. The small units are balanced with ceilings that are higher than usual, bi-level plans, and individual terraces on the upper levels. The units are composed of surplus windows and doors, scrap materials from the metal industry and are clad with a transparent, corrugated plastic panels.

ADAM KALKIN
12 CONTAINER HOUSE
Brooklin, Maine, USA

The 12 Container House is a custom prefabricated house created from twelve recycled shipping containers. This T-shaped two-storey summer home features floor-to-ceiling windows, concrete floors, two fireplaces, and radiant in-floor heating.

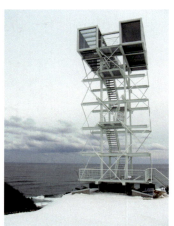

BUREAU DES MÉSARCHITECTURES
Didier Fiuza Faustino
SKY IS THE LIMIT
Yang Yang, South Korea

This tea pavilion by Bureau des
Mésarchitectures is exemplary in
its approach to summoning up art
from architecture and architecture
from art.

ROSS STEVENS
CONTAINER HOUSE
Wellington, New Zealand

CASTOR DESIGN
SAUNA BOX

Toronto and northern Ontario, Canada

For the Sauna Box, Castor Design have turned a conventional shipping container into a self-contained traditional sauna with solar power and a stereo, solar panels, and a wood-fired stove.

CONTAINERART

1 | Fabio Niccolini
DA GRANDE FARÒ L'ARTISTA
Pegli, Italy

Container Art is an urban, itinerant, and adaptive art exhibit. Installations, sculptures, and paintings by innovative talents from the local and global artscape are displayed in many containers spread around town. A different work of contemporary art is shown in each container, and a different mix of artists in each city. Here, for example, the artist Fabio Niccolini positioned a container on a pier so the viewer could contemplate the sea either by looking inside the container, or by turning the other way.

CONTAINERART

2 | Red Art-L. Amato
OXIGENUS
Rome, Italy

Oxigenus is the description of a future world in which oxygen will be a scarce commodity. The installation is an immersive experience in a sad and not so improbable world.

CONTAINERART

3 | Davide Ragazzi
MODULI LUNARI
Genova-Rome, Italy

A potpourri of lines, numbers, and light positioned in unlikely places on the outskirts of Genova and, later, in the centre of Rome.

CONTAINERART

4 | Nicola Villa
PRESSURE
Genova, Italy

5 | Carmen Einfinger
CONTAINER COZY
Genova, Italy

PHOOEY ARCHITECTS
CHILDREN'S ACTIVITY CENTRE
Skinners Adventure Playground,
South Melbourne, Australia

Four shipping containers were
transformed into a Children's
Activity Centre, located at Skinners
Playground in Melbourne, Australia.
The form and aesthetics were generated by sustainable strategies aimed
at zero waste. When the reused containers were joined in a staggered
arrangement, intimate and public
spaces were created for a variety of
functions, including study, painting,
dancing, and lounging about. Each
container was oriented to produce
visual and physical connections to
surrounding playground spaces.
Rainwater from the containers drains
into a pond and reed bed. All materials brought to the site were durable,
recycled, reclaimed, reused, or
salvaged from demolition.

47

SOU FOUJIMOTO ARCHITECTS
HOUSE O
Chiba, Japan

A weekend house located on a rocky coast that is a two hours' drive from Tokyo. The site is a rocky stretch facing the Pacific Ocean, with approaches sloping down to the water. The shape of this single continuous room spreads out like the branches of a tree. All the required spaces – an entrance, living area, dining area, kitchen, bedroom, Japanese-style room, study room, and bathroom – are arranged in this one continuous space. Oriented in different directions, visitors can find various views of the ocean when walking through the house.

SOU FOUJIMOTO ARCHITECTS
HOUSE N
Oita, Japan

This minimalist residence in Oita Japan by Sou Fujimoto Architects is composed of a small residence-scaled volume encased in a larger, more urban-scale structure. The larger structure is subtracted asymmetrically, creating a range of experiential moments in the interstitial space around the enclosed dwelling. These subtractions also create a variety of experiences in the more controlled, glassed-in volume. This series of nesting boxes is transparent, even as it is smartly layered to create privacy where needed.

page 52

OBSERVATORIUM
Geert van de Camp, Andre Dekker,
Ruud Reutelingsperger
PAVILION FÜR ZECHE ZOLLVEREIN
Essen, Germany

As part of a park design for the
UNESCO world heritage site Zollverein in the Ruhr area, six pavilions
will be built at the entrances of the
very large site, using materials and
scales that blend into the garden city
around the Zollverein. Measurements:
sixteen metres long, eight metres
wide, and four metres high.

RACHEL WHITEREAD
HOUSE
London, UK

Perhaps one of Rachel Whiteread's
best known works, House is a concrete cast of the inside of an entire
Victorian terraced house, exhibited
at the location of the original house
in East London.

CHAPTER 02

LET'S PLAY HOUSE

GO HASEGAWA & ASSOCIATES

TUMBLEWEED TINY HOUSE COMPANY

Reconstructing mankind's archetypal dwelling remains perhaps the most prevalent leitmotiv in architectural theory and building practice to this day. Indeed, for centuries the search for the untraceable primitive hut has been one of architecture's eternal quests.

Let's Play House introduces the reader to numerous formalistic modifications of this elementary form of dwelling. Four plain walls and a pitched roof – reminiscent in their simplicity of a child's drawing – become the subject here of various humorous transformations. This game with the basic design of architectural principles can be found in Alexander Konstantinov's colourful house-wrappings or Gregor Passen's overturned, corrugated-iron house, which is slightly suggestive of a tank, as well as in Nathan Coley's blackened Western-style Saloon and Ai Weiwei's ironic and storey-spanning submersion of a house into the ground – to mention only a few. But whereas these projects can be regarded as ingenious artistic takes on the ancestral hut, numerous technical adaptations of this perennial structure can also be found in this chapter. These range from Jonas Wagell's prefabricated, flat-pack delivery Mini House, which requires no more than a weekend to assemble, and Studio Mama's cedar-shingle-clad Beach House to Cheng + Snyder's monolithic Writer's Block at the mouth of Sheepscott River in Westport, Maine, or Aoki Jun's House N, a two-storey white cube adorned with a pitched roof, chimney, and mullioned windows.

All in all, this chapter vividly demonstrates the broad versatility of even the most primitive spatial design.

HOUSE IN THE CLOUDS

1 | **RICHARD WILSON**
18 HOLES
Folkestone, UK

The proposal for this project at the Folkestone Triennial 2008 outlines the construction of beach huts along the sea front. The huts are cut from concrete slabs that made up the abandoned 18 Hole, a crazy golf course located at the back of the esplanade. The exterior surfaces hark back, in colour and form, to the golfing game.

2 | **OSKAR LEO KAUFMANN &**
JOHANNES NORLANDER
HOUSES A & B
Milano, Italy

Presented for the first time, at Salone del Mobile, this house by Norlander and Kaufmann is not a design experiment but an innovative approach towards modern housing. The basic models come with or without water, electricity, or heating. The buyer can add colour, as well as supplementary equipment offered in various packages, such as additional windows and doors, shutters, or solar cells.

**BRUT DELUXE
KIOSK M.POLI**
Madrid, Spain

This kiosk was conceived for temporary street markets or handicraft fairs. It is not meant as an individual object, but as part of a whole that builds up a small village – a little world of its own fitted into the city. When closed, the kiosk is a volume covered by a double roof, a house in its most minimal expression. When opened, a transformation starts. Part of its façade can be rotated onto the roof, giving the kiosk a more vertical and striking proportion.

FULGURO
TERRASSE NESTLÉ
Montreux, Canada

For the Montreux Jazz Festival, Nestlé comissioned the Swiss designers Fulguro to create a space bar and restaurant on the docks in Montreux. The temporary terrace was open during the two weeks of the festival.

Fulguro designed a platform built between the docks and the lake, ending in bleachers. The bar's form is reminiscent of a beach hut. A large section of the house is raised, like the lid of a cardboard packaging box, and generates a sheltered area for customers waiting to be served.

GO HASEGAWA & ASSOCIATES
HOUSE IN A FOREST
Nagano, Japan

**JONAS WAGELL DESIGN &
ARCHITECTURE**
MINI HOUSE
Katrineholm, Sweden

This prefabricated, flat-pack delivery Mini House by Jonas Wagell can be assembled on a weekend. It is a modern, functional, and attractive fifteen-square-metre Swedish friggebod shed, suited for both summer and winter living. In addition to the small house, the concept provides an outdoor terrace with a pergola, all within the framework of permit-free Swedish building regulations. Furthermore, Mini House can be customised with add-ons such as kitchen and bath modules, a heater-kit with a chimney, or a solar power unit to provide the house with electricity.

page 61

MAURER UNITED ARCHITECTS [MUA]
GUESTHOUSE BELVÉDÈRE
Maastricht, Netherlands

Maastricht-based Maurer United
Architects designed a folly on
Belvédère Mountain, the former
rubbish dump of the municipality of
Maastricht. The mountain offers a
fascinating view of Maastricht from

the rear. The view is exploited in the
design by two large vantage windows, which direct the visitor's gaze
towards the city on the one side and
to the cultural and historical heritage
of the Belvédère natural area on the
other. When the windows are closed,
one can still view the sky by looking
straight up through the roof window.

VIA GRAFIK
GARDEN HOUSE
Wiroclaw, Poland

Via Grafik's Garden House is an
ironic take on German allotment garden culture and its idea of protecting
and delimiting one's property. The
sculpture exaggerates this intention
by having no use for its owner.

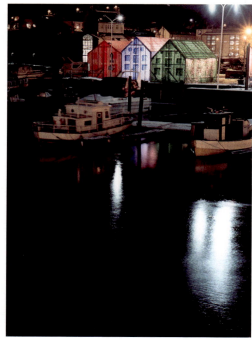

ALEKSANDER KONSTANTINOV

1 | **LIGHT IN NOVEMBER**
Trondheim, Norway

A project realised during the
artist's stay at the Lademoen
Kunstnerverksteder residency with
support of the Trondheim Kommune
and the Norwegian University of
Science and Technology.

2 | **LE QUARTIER**
Quimper, France

A three-part installation created at
the suggestion of the Le Quartier
Centre of Contemporary Art in
Quimper.

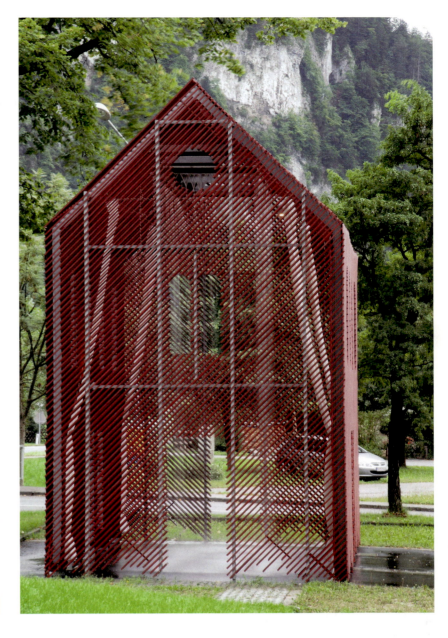

ALEKSANDER KONSTANTINOV

3 | **HAUS UNTER DER LINDE**
Hohenems, Austria

A project commissioned by the private
museum Otten Kunst Raum on the
occasion of its opening.

4 | **VILLA BERNASCONI**
Lancy, Geneva

A work created upon invitation by the
Service culturel de Lancy during the
artist's residency at Villa Bernasconi.

1 | **KUMIKO INUI**
SHIN–YATSUSHIRO MONUMENT
Yatsushiro Japan

This is a house-shaped pavilion with a triangular plan; there are multiple square holes of different sizes punched in the walls and roof.

2 | **FRANZ HÖFNER & HARRY SACHS**
GREENHOUSE MODEL RIGA
Riga, Latvia

OBSERVATORIUM
Geert van de Camp, Andre Dekker,
Ruud Reutelingsperger
HALLENHAUS
Neukirchen-Vluyn, Germany

Hallenhaus, by Rotterdam-based
Observatorium, is a large steel
sculpture on a slag-heap near
the motorway in the Ruhr area
of Germany. It is a landmark of
transformation from industrial to
recreational, a place of silent retreat
and a link to the architectural history
of the region.

The House and The Tree is a mixed-media installation about the natural and the man-made, the urban and the rural, the personal and the public. O'Kane re-created an attic from his family home, into which he placed a short film recording the vernacular architecture of Co. Donegal, which is accompanied by a soundtrack of proverbs in Gaelic. The installation is completed by a large-scale wall-drawing of an oak tree that once sheltered King James II, and by the sawn up trunk of this tree, which was struck by lightning.

NATHAN COLEY
PALACE
Haunch of Venison, Berlin, Germany

Coley's work breaks down our ideas and perceptions of space and the built environment, exploring our relationships to political borders, religious frontiers and ideals, analysing our investment and claims on architecture as well as on public and private spaces. As per a real film set, the 1880s-style Western façade of a saloon and bar front is six metres high and stained entirely black.

Signs over the three 'building' fronts have been removed and replaced instead with the words WEALTH, BELIEF, LAND, MIND, LIFE – the five rights that every human is granted under Islam.

**AI WEIWEI
IN BETWEEN**
Installation SOHO, Beijing, China

For this piece commissioned by
the Soho New Town Condominium,
Chinese architect Ai Weiwei installed a heavy concrete structure
suspended in an atrium – alluding
to Chinese developers' penchant for
ruthless demolition.

**GREGOR PASSENS
CATERPILLAR**
Germany

MICHAEL BEUTLER
ALUMINIUM PAGODA
Frankfurt/Main, Germany

For this project, Michael Beutler erected an aluminium pagoda-like tower in one of the greened atriums of the Lufthansa Aviation Center.

page 69/1,2,3
TUMBLEWEED TINY HOUSE COMPANY
Jay Shafer
1 | **WEEBEE**
California, USA

2 | **EPU**
California, USA

Worried about the impact a large house would have on the environment, Jay Shafer founded Tumbleweed Tiny Houses in 1997. The EPU is the house Jay Shafer lives in. It comes with a desk and fireplace in the main room; a kitchen; wet bath; and loft upstairs.

3 | **XS-HOUSE**
California, USA

The XS-House is the smallest house Tumbleweed Tiny House Company offers. It has two closets that flank the front door, a heater, and a sleeping loft above.

HOUSE IN THE CLOUDS
HOUSE IN THE CLOUDS
Thorpeness, Suffolk, UK

Set on one acre of private grounds, the House in the Clouds provides spacious accommodation for family holidays.

LOY BOWLIN
BEAUTIFUL HOLY JEWEL HOME
McComb, Mississippi, USA

Aiming to style himself as a singing 'rhinestone cowboy' modelled after Glen Campbell's song, Loy Bowlin of McComb, Mississippi, became the creator of a remarkable art environment. To boost his spirits, he turned a brightly coloured suit into a painted and festooned glamour costume and headed for town with his harmonica.

He enjoyed the laughter and attention the decorated suit received, and he quickly became known as the 'The Original Rhinestone Cowboy'. His persona needed a backdrop, and thus he embellished his small home with glitter cut paper, magazine pictures, ornaments, and spangles. After Bowlin's death, the house was slated for demolition, but was saved, virtually at the last minute, in front of the wrecking crew and dismantled piece by piece. Today, the preserved Holy Jewel Home stands inside the John Michael Kohler Arts Center gallery and, along with many of Bowlin's fancy suits, hats, and furniture, is the only comprehensively relocated environment in the permanent collection.

SUMER EREK
THE NEWSPAPER HOUSE
London, UK

The Newspaper House is a participatory public art project installed at Gillet Square, Hackney, London in spring 2008. The house is built of used newspapers, plastic cable ties, and wood.

JONAS LIVERÖD
IMMACULATE CATHEDRAL FOR THE
LAST DAYS OF A STAVANGER VISION
Rogaland Centre of Art, Stavanger, Norway

Built out of leftover materials from the city, the Immaculate Cathedral was built around a large church-like window at the Rogaland Centre of Art. As a site-specific installation, cathedral, DJ-hut, and place for socialising, it brought the people of the city together for relaxed talks about the future of culture in Stavanger.

TILL GERHARD
HELTER SKELTER SHELTER
Galerie Michael Janssen, Berlin,
Germany

GERDA STEINER & JÖRG LENZLINGER
THE MYSTERY OF FERTILITY
Sonsbeek, Arnhem, Netherlands

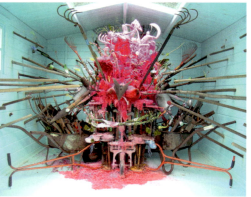

HERBERT & MASON, KSUBI
THE BOMBE MACHE
Melbourne, Australia

This store was designed and created by Herbert Mason Architects
together with Ksubi. Meant to reflect
the impermanence of retail design,
the store follows the brand's 'anti'
theme with an anti-retail therapy
aesthetic. Eighty per cent of the
shop is constructed from refuse
and throw-away materials. The
entire construction is customised
and handcrafted to render materials beyond recognition or original
expectations.

STUDIO JAN HABRAKEN &
ALISSIA MELKA TEICHROEW
PEEL EXHITIBION
Peel Gallery Houston, Texas, USA

For an exhibition at Peel Gallery by
studio Jan Habraken and byAMT, the
artists sliced up a house into separate sections: a Studio Jan Habraken
part, with unique objects mixed
with prototypes and manufactured
objects, and a byAMT part, which
shows prototypes and products
made in recent years. The last house
is called the 'shop' as this is where
the artists' manufactured products
are shown and sold.

**HÜTTEN & PALÄSTE /
G.D.HOLZFREUNDE B.R.
LAUBE GRZEGORZEWSKI**
Berlin, Germany

**I-BEAM DESIGN
PALLET HOUSE**
Architecture Triennale, Milan, Italy

The Pallet House, by I-Beam Design, was conceived as a transitional shelter for refugees. There was a need for an alternative to the typical tent solution – one that could transform temporary living conditions into a permanent home. It is an inexpensive and efficient solution to the problem of housing people displaced by natural disasters, plagues, famine, political and economic strife, or war. Versatile, recyclable, sustainable, easily assembled, and inexpensive, wooden shipping pallets are the principal building module.

STUDIOMAMA
BEACH CHALET
Whitstable, Kent, England

The Beach Chalet structure is built on galvanised steel stilts to prevent flooding. The outside of the chalet is clad with cedar shingles, and the inside with sawn softwood. Because the land slopes away from the beach, both internal and external steps were constructed to create a level surface inside.

Adding height to the rear of the chalet meant that there was space for a mezzanine level, which now serves as a sleeping platform, with an oblong-shaped window above it providing beautiful views of the countryside. Behind the kitchen are the children's bunk beds and the bathroom. The sea view is the focus of this simple living space.

JOOST AKKERMANS
CAMPING RAFT
Utrecht, Netherlands

The Camping Raft consists of sturdy tree trunks, floating safely in barrels, with a wooden hut.

page 76
CHENG+SNYDER
WRITER'S BLOCK I
Westport Island, Maine, USA

Located at the mouth of the Sheepscott River in Westport, Maine, this new structure combines two functions: that of a writing studio and that of a boat house. An interlocking programme and allocating a double function to design elements are the concepts behind this small 'block'. Canoe storage = combination workspace + bed. Interior structure = book + utility shelving.

The windows and awning are arranged to maximise views and allow passive heating and cooling. These elements were 'carved' out of the traditional saltwater barn form, animating the exterior, but allowing a peaceful interior. The monolithic form with concealed corner doors and punctured corner windows adds a mysterious quality to this tranquil retreat.

KASBAH–HÄUSER
University of Art & Design Helsinki
& Kunsthochschule Kassel
HOUSE MAARIT
Kassel, Germany

Haus Maarit is one of the five temporary guesthouses built for documenta 12 in Kassel. In the small guesthouse designed by Maarit Eskola, a student at the Helsinki University of Art and Design, the atmosphere is similar to that in a birch copse where growth has become frenzied.

**JÜRGEN HEINERT,
MICHAEL SAILSTORFER
3 STER MIT AUSBLICK**
Germany

Michael Sailstorfer and Jürgen
Heinert allow a stand-alone wooden
hut to fall victim to its own stove in
this project.

1 | **ALEKSANDER KONSTANTINOV**
IZBA, BASILICA
Nicolo-Lenivez, Kaluga Area, Russia

pages 30 / 2, 81
SKENE CATLING DE LA PENA
THE DAIRY HOUSE
Hadspen Estate, Somerset, UK

The Dairy House by London-based architect Skene Catling de la Peña is a dairy in Somerset, England, that was converted into a five-bedroom house. Rather than demolishing and rebuilding, the sense of 'retreat' was to be reinforced through 'camouflage'. The form and massing of the extension echo and complement the existing structure.

JUN AOKI & ASSOCIATES
HOUSE N
Yokohama, Kanagawa, Japan

This two-storey block adorned with a pitched roof, brick chimney, and mullioned windows by Tokyo Architect Jun Aoki faces the street and offers a large wooden dock in the back.

BENJAMÍN MURÚA ARCHITECTS & CONSTANZA INFANTE S
COUNTRYSIDE HOUSE
Curacaví, Chile

The objective of this project was to reuse and emphasise some elements of Chilean houses from the early twentieth century, such as patios, galleries, and open corridors, which are also present in the pre-existing building. The building is set on a plain overlooking hills to the east and a valley to the west. The configuration of the house made it possible to work with open corridors, galleries, and patios that work like filters between the building and the landscape.

KALHÖFER–KORSCHILDGEN
FAHRT INS GRÜNE
Lüttringhausen, Germany

This mobile extension of a traditional half-timbered house connects the building with the garden and reacts to seasonal changes. In the summer, the annex building moves aside and uncovers a terrace. In the winter, when the terrace is no longer needed, the building slides back and conjoins with the house.

JOHN KÖRMELING
ROTATING HOUSE
Tilburg, Netherlands

Dutch artist John Körmeling places a detached terraced house with a front and back yard on a roundabout in the city of Tilburg. The house, which looks real, rotates on the roundabout in the direction of the traffic and completes one full round in twenty hours, causing drivers to feel alienated.

pages 85 - 87
ADAM KALKIN
BUNNY LANE
Bernardsville, New Jersey, USA

Architect Adam Kalkin's Bunny Lane
House is an industrial shed built
around a traditional two-storey house
in New Jersey. Its remnants are still
visible throughout the new building.

CHAPTER 03

WHEN NATURE CALLS

TREEHOUSE CREATIONS

WORK ARCHITECTURE COMPANY

For some time now, all lights have switched to green. A new worldwide awareness of our natural environment's vulnerability is setting the stage for active change. Sustainability and global warming have become the focus of heated debates in a range of media, from sober (and sobering) scientific publications to high-gloss trend and lifestyle magazines.

The chapter When Nature Calls devotes itself to the subject of ecological change, showcasing a panoply of projects that respond to nature's call for sustainability in a variety of fitting as well as ironic ways. Ton Matton's mobile nature reserve, for instance, was a bus, covered in greenery, that travelled the roads of Rotterdam during the International Architecture Biennial. The vehicle served as a moving platform for architects, city planners, ecologists, and biologists, facilitating discussions on the relationship between culture and nature in and around the city. Another example can be found in Work Architecture's Urban Farm installation, a magical plot of rural delights incorporated into the city grid and shown at the P.S.1 Contemporary Art Center in New York City. An abundance of exotic, off-track sites are to be found in this chapter as well, encompassing everything from dreamy tree-houses by Baumraum, Roderick Romero, or Yuichi Kobayashi to a curious sheep pen by Dutch architects 70F, a zeppelin-shaped house on a wooded Australian mountainside by Bellemo & Cat, or a weekend house with a looping hallway by Atelier Tekuto.

Here, it quickly becomes clear that sustainable architecture has succeeded, within a generation, in moving away from decades of alien existence and into the mainstream. The eco-banality of its outward appearance has since given way to design concepts as creative as they are aesthetically demanding.

TERUNOBU FUJIMORI, KEIICHI KAWAKAMI

OLIVER BISHOP-YOUNG
SKIP WASTE – WATER GARDEN
London, UK

This project involves converting
empty skips around the city into
public spaces such as skate parks,
swimming pools, and gardens.

1 | REBAR
PARKCYCLE
San Francisco, USA

The PARKcycle is a human-powered, open-space distribution system designed for agility within the existing automobile-centred city environment. Using a plug-and-play approach, the PARKcycle provides open-space benefits to neighbour-hoods that need it, when they need it, as soon as it is parked.

2 | KEVIN VAN BRAAK
CARAVAN 01
Vlissingen, Netherlands

This caravan does not appear to be different from any other caravan when it is pulled behind a car; when opened, however, it transforms into an artificial garden, park, or camping site. Inside the caravan, there are stuffed animals, artificial grass, silk flowers and trees, a sound installation with bird sounds, and a barbecue.

MATTONOFFICE
MOBILE NATURE RESERVE
Rotterdam, Netherlands

This Mobile Nature Reserve travelled the roads of Rotterdam during the International Architecture Biennial 2003. Debates and dialogues took place in the bus en route, with architects, city planners, ecologists, and biologists hammering out the relations between culture and nature in and around the city of Rotterdam. As the bus visited selected locations, standpoints were argued and demonstrated.

1 | **VACANT LOT**
Hoxton, London, UK

A formerly inaccessible and run-down plot of housing estate land was transformed into a beautiful oasis of green. Seventy half-tonne bags of soil were arranged to form an allotment space. Within their individual plots, local residents carefully tend a spectacular array of vegetables, salads, fruits, and flowers, helping a new sense of community to emerge.

2 | **TRAVELLING SHED**
Staines, Surrey, UK

For three weeks the SHED advertised the beauty of a productive plot or a wildlife habitat in property development style. Don't mow it, grow it! In March 2006 a shed from a Surrey garden appeared in the shopping centre of Farnham, Esher, and Staines, where free digital garden makeovers were offered to local residents.

3 | **2A+P ARCHITETTURA**
I LOVE GREEN
Rome, Italy

For the White Nights event in Rome, 2A+P architettura redesigned Piazza Capranica as a labyrinthine relaxation area and natural landscape. The materials used to build I LOVE GREEN were chosen because of their ability to avoid environmental waste for a night-long event.

**CHRISTOPH KLEMMT,
HAJIME MURAMATSU & SVEN STEINER
WITH SHIN EGASHIRA
STAR-SPOTTING FOLLY**
Koshirakura, Niigata Prefecture, Japan

This folly for observing the stars was built in Koshirakura, Niigata Prefecture, Japan. It was designed for the local residents, who have a strong interest in star-gazing, especially for their parent-and-child playgroup. The small-scale observatory was built in the darkest spot in the village, on a hill behind the local school, which is also one of the points closest to the night sky. A concrete foundation was laid to position a telescope in precise alignment with the constellations. A staircase affixed to a wall leads up to a seat to watch shooting stars. This block can be rotated in the direction of meteorite showers, which are marked on the base of the observatory. On windy nights, the staircase block and the wall to which it is affixed can be opened to act as shields against wind and light when the telescope is being used.

OBSERVATORIUM
Geert van de Camp, Andre Dekker,
Ruud Reutelingsperger
EPICENTRUM
Krasnoyarsk, Russia

A bookcase studio supported by wooden beams in front of the city museum is used for a moment of retreat and reflection. It was part of an exhibition and symposium about the psychological and mystifying effects of the Tungaska event, a powerful explosion, caused by the airburst of a large meteor, that occurred near the Podkamennaya Tunguska River in Russia in 1908.

1 | **MARJETICA POTRČ**
FOREST RISING

The Curve, Barbican Art Gallery,
London, UK

Forest Rising is an island community
floating on some forty tree trunks,
including a field, pier, helicopter
platform, and a school, complete
with solar panels and a satellite dish.
As a powerful evocation of Amazonian
life in the twenty-first century, it
focuses on a commendable local
response to deforestation and rising

water levels. On the one hand, the
work inevitably points to the dangers
of globalisation, climate change, and
unsustainable urban growth. On the
other hand, Forest Rising shows how
rural living can offer a model for the
future – a vibrant community that
is both self-supporting and globally
connected.

2 | **KRISTIN POSEHN**
ROOT

Winchester, England

The installation Root functioned like a
vacant lot, which viewers were free
to explore. A footpath at the gallery
entrance wound its way through the
installation and led through double-
doors to the parking bay at the rear.
The work was created on site over a
period of several months, and by the
time of its completion had become
a mini-ecosystem of growth and
decomposition.

page 97
BENJAMIN VERDONCK
NEST ROTTERDAM
Rotterdam, Netherlands

The artist built a giant, human-sized nest on the side of the Weena skyscraper in Rotterdam. Nest Rotterdam hangs fifty metres above the street and was constructed in six weeks.

3 | **GUY BEN-NER**
TREEHOUSE KIT
Venice Biennial, Venice, Italy

This piece was originally conceived as an installation for the Israeli pavilion at the 2005 Venice Biennial. It consists of a video movie and a sculptural tree, made of furniture. The movie is a 'manual' with an instructor – a crossover between an IKEA salesman, a Jewish settler, and Robinson Crusoe – demonstrating step by step how to create a home out of a tree, a country out of an island. It is a story that starts with a unique object – a tree, a piece of art – and ends up as a few very common pieces of furniture, which together create a home.

1 | **PATRICK DOUGHERTY**
DOIN' THE LOCOMOTION
Grounds for Sculpture, Hamilton, New Jersey, USA

2 | **BENJAMIN VERDONCK**
BRONKS
Antwerp, Belgium

PHOEBE WASHBURN
TICKLE THE SHITSTEM
Zach Feuer Gallery, New York, USA

Phoebe Washburn's work explores generative systems based on absurd patterns of production. In Tickle the Shitstem, Washburn has developed a system/environment in which production and waste are equally important. The Shitstem generates its own products along with the inevitable by-products or waste, and at times, there is little or no distinction between the two. The installation simply keeps churning, producing, and haemorrhaging cyclically unless it is interrupted by a failure. Products of Tickle the Shitstem include beverages, pencils, coloured urchins, and t-shirts.

GERDA STEINER & JÖRG LENZLINGER
THE INVADERS
Botanical Garden, Geneva,
Switzerland

Plants that manage to become
established on new territory are
called invader plants. For biologists,
such plants are a thorn in the flesh
because they harass the indigenous
flora in the last remaining small
wilderness. For this project, Gerda
Steiner and Jörg Lenzlinger transformed a travel-weary container
into a greenhouse in which the same
conditions (earth, light, water, and
loving care) prevail for all plants.
These include invader plants, vegetables, flowers, weeds, indoor plants,
herbs, creepers of all kinds, artificial
plants, almost extinct grasses, and
thriving fertiliser crystals growing in
suitcases, handbags, and shoes.

GERDA STEINER & JÖRG LENZLINGER
LE MÉTA-JARDIN
La Maison Rouge, Paris, France

In the Méta Jardin, the biodiversity
of colourful junk meets the biodiversity of brilliant exclusivity. Growing
and decomposing structures live in
the same territories hand in hand.
Values dissolve. A dense vegetation
after the big crash! Aloe vera grows
near a used motor oil lake with a
mushroom island. Creepers twine up
a tangle of cables. Roots turn into
tubes. Moments of attraction alternate with moments of rejection.

WORK ARCHITECTURE COMPANY
PUBLIC FARM 1
PS1 Contemporary Art Center,
New York, USA

Since 1999, New York's Museum of Modern Art and its sister institution, the PS1 Contemporary Art Center, have been hosting the Young Architects Program to design a temporary installation in the courtyards of PS1 in Queens, New York, for their summer warm-up parties. The winning project in 2008 was Work Architecture's Public Farm 1 (P.F.1). It is an urban farming project and a playful architectural and urban manifesto to reinvent our cities, and our world.

The temporary installation is an attempt to bring the qualities of the countryside into the city by growing fruit and vegetables in large cardboard tubes above a communal area. Fifty-one varieties of herbs, fruits, and vegetables were selected to thrive in the urban environment and planted to bloom in succession throughout the summer.

SANEI HOPKINS ARCHITECTS
MOBILE ECO SECOND HOME
(M.E.S.H.)
Suffolk, UK

In this playful second family home, Sanie Hopkins Architects created a space that consists of five bunk beds stacked vertically for the children with a double bunk on top for the parents. The space under the double bunk creates the main horizontal circulation route through the structure. Originally inspired by stratospheric bombers and tactical nuclear submarines, this structure provides a very compact and economical home away from home.

SANEI HOPKINS ARCHITECTS
GARDEN ROOM
Suffolk, UK

The Garden Room is inspired by Wold War II pillboxes for the home defence forces; these had been designed specifically for long periods of contemplation and reflection by the individuals who operated them. This project was conceived as a space for just one person to contemplate and work.

MICHEL DE BROIN
SUPERFICIAL
Vosges, Alsace, France

To reflect on the notion of transparency, Michel de Broin enveloped the contours of a large stone with fragments of mirror. The stone, tucked away deep in the woods, became a reflective surface for its surroundings. In this play of splintered radiance, the rock disappears in its reflections.

GARDEN PAVILION
Sant Miquel de Cruïlles, Girona, Spain

This compact winter storage unit unfolds into an open inhabitable space during the warmer months. A system of sliding/folding doors and windows opens the storeroom to the garden. The pavilion was built as a piece of furniture, with great attention to detail. The scheme adopts a fragmented geometry that encourages the visitor to walk around the structure; it refuses to reveal its volume, offering a different view from every corner of the garden.

2 | **ULLMAYER SYLVESTER**
THE NEW SUMMERHOUSE
London, UK

This surprising summerhouse in a narrow back yard in London is made of wood, plastic, and mirror-foil.

page 105
GIANNI BOTSFORD ARCHITECTS
CASA KIKE
Cahuita, Costa Rica

Reappraising the architectural heritage of the region and reviving indigenous techniques, Gianni Botsford Architects created an eco-architecture that impacts only minimally, both physically and environmentally. The main structure rests on a timber base, raised on stilts. These are set on small concrete pad foundations poured into individual pits. The load-bearing element of the two pavilion-like buildings is an intricate pattern of diagonal timber beams and columns. The shape of the two pavilions reacts to the environmental results: it assists in promoting the best views and ventilation while keeping the low sunlight out of the interior spaces and screening them off from neighbouring properties.

SSD
VERDANT STUDIOS
Athens, Vermont, USA

This recording studio, created by Single Speed Design for a renowned recording engineer and musician, solves specific issues of acoustics while engaging the site and context. As an extension of an existing century-old barn, the new structure uses a pitched roof: a simple 'scissor' truss is mirrored to create both an east and west skylight, while on the interior, the asymmetrical space allows for a positive scattering of sound. The open end-bay of the structure telescopes views into the rural landscape and creates a rest area for musicians.

TOMMIE WILHELMSEN
HEATHER HOUSE
Rogaland, Norway

Heather House is named after the landscape in which it is located. Heather and birch dominate the landscape with the mountains as background. The house has been placed in the terrain without altering the natural surroundings.

RB ARKITEKTUR
Rahel Belatchew Arkitektur
VILLA RBDVD
Stockholm, Sweden

The RBDVD-house is a commentary on the tradition of wooden single family houses in Sweden. Here, the highly standardised prefabricated industry has formed not only the construction process, but also the architectural expression. The wooden construction is character-ised by a simple and clearly defined structure and division of space, as part of which the proportions of the plan, the façade, and the internal subdivisions are interrelated through repetitions and changes in scale of an initial rectangular form.

ATELIER TEKUTO
MEBIUS HOUSE
Kamakura, Japan

A ten-minute drive away from Kamakura, the Mebius House is surrounded by part of the mountain range to the west of the city. Atelier Tekuto developed the theme for the building based on various rhythms and wavelengths, such as those of the sun, lunar cycles, and plant and human life. The building's space is a fusion of interior and exterior layer-like elements. The plans specifically called for a corridor that forms a square, accompanied by other spaces of complementary volumes.

1 | SAMI RINTALA
FOREST OBSERVATORY
Kirishima, Kyushu, Japan

The Kirishima outdoor museum, with its permanent exhibition including sculptures and spatial art works, is located in the rainforest of Kyushu Island, Japan. Here Sami Rintala was invited to design a new work for the museum area, with the only condition being that the work should last for at least three hundred years. The observation station is a spatial instrument that helps visitors listen to and sense the surrounding nature more keenly. The walls around the pavilion catch sounds from different directions while the courtyard is, acoustically, a more protected space for meetings and conversation.

2 | ARCHEA ASSOCIATI
SAN VINCENZO CAMPING
San Vincenzo, Italy

San Vincenzo Camping, designed by Archea Associati, is located in an area of particularly beautiful landscape on the Etruscan coast of Italy. The project was planned for the area and includes large green spaces, plots for tents and bungalows, group spaces for recreation, sports and gathering, and service spaces to offer its guests comfortable stays. The architecture is almost primitive – as simple as it is sophisticated in its attention to details. At night, the architecture changes its image without altering it, becoming a diaphanous partition of colour and light.

CHRISTIAN POTTGIESSER /
ARCHITECTURESPOSSIBLES
HUOT EN PONS
Paris, France

A nineteenth-century factory hall has found a new lease of life as the Paris headquarters of the companies PONS and HUOT. It was restored completely back to its original state. Most of the space the architects were asked to create is accommodated within a box of solid oak that spans the entire interior. Stamped into its surface are individual workstations, equipped with a Plexiglas telephone hood. The interior of the new structure houses conference rooms and communal rooms. Eight Ficus Panda trees grow through the space, their lush green foliage improving the quality of the interior climate. Individual offices are housed on the mezzanine gallery of the factory hall.

1 | **ISAY WEINFELD**
CASA D'ÁGUA
São Paulo, Brazil

The defining element of this project by
Brazilian architect Isay Weinfeld is a
narrow pool that runs from the street
door alongside the house, for the
whole length of the land: in the first
half, large granite stones anchored
to the bottom slab skip across the
water surface forming a pathway to
the central patio; further, it becomes
a swimming lane that stretches to
the back wall of the plot. Outside,
thick natural-twine ropes make up
a curtain that shadows the patio and
filters the sunlight.

pages 112/2, 113
HUSOS
GBHNPCB
Cali, Colombia

In South America, the Madrid-based
architecture practice Husos designed
the prototype for a garden building,
covered in host and nectar plants,
in Cali, Colombia. As part of an urban
reclamation project on an ecological
model, this housing unit was designed to attract and sustain Cali's
butterflies, acting as a biometer in a
sensitive natural habitat undergoing
unprecedented development. At the
same time, it houses living and production spaces, as well as a shop for
Taller Croquis, a small design atelier
in a central area of Cali.

page 114
**TERUNOBU FUJIMORI,
KEIICHI KAWAKAMI
CHARRED CEDAR HOUSE**
Nagano, Japan

This house is situated on a family estate located in a residential area of Nagano City. The themes of the project are the Japanese chestnut and the cave. Inside the building, the walls, ceiling, and floor are covered with Japanese chestnut. The house, viewed from the outside, looks like a cave.

page 115
**TERUNOBU FUJIMORI,
YOSHIAKI IRIE
LAMUNE HOT SPRING HOUSE**
Oita, Japan

For this hot spring of carbonated water, three public spas – a men's, a women's, and a family bath – were constructed to face a courtyard covered with bamboo grasses. The walls consist of black and white stripes made of charred cedar and white plaster. The roofs are made of sheet copper bent by hand. Pine trees are planted on top of the roofs.

**SCHOOL OF ARCHITECTURE,
UNIVERSIDAD DE TALCA, CHILE**
1 | Ingrid Vega
BOX IN CANELLILLO
Canelillo, Chile

**SCHOOL OF ARCHITECTURE,
UNIVERSIDAD DE TALCA, CHILE**
2 | Ronald Hernandez, Marcelo Valdes,
Osvaldo Veliz
**LANDMARK: TOURISTIC RURAL
CIRCUIT, DRYLANDS**
Rauco, Chepica, Lolol, Hualañe,
Vichuquén.

This project traces a route through the Chilean coastal mountain range, which runs along the Pacific Ocean on the west and the Central Valley on the east. Existing ancient paths are the only infrastructure available for reaching this area called 'the drylands'. Seven modules have been built along the route, each serving as a means of orientation and as resting areas for tourists.

**SCHOOL OF ARCHITECTURE,
UNIVERSIDAD DE TALCA, CHILE**
3 | Blanca Azocar Andrade
PAVILION LABORERS PSICULTURA
Bramadero, Chile

**SCHOOL OF ARCHITECTURE,
UNIVERSIDAD DE TALCA, CHILE**
4 | Claudio Castillo Moscoso
PAVILION RACING 'TO THE CHILEAN'
Gualleco, Chile

70F ARCHITECTURE
SHEEP STABLE
Almere, Netherlands

This sheep stable is designed to enable the public or school classes to visit the building and experience the care and breeding of sheep up close. At one end of the building, on the second floor, a room for the shepherd and a small office have been created. There are sleeping facilities for the shepherd, who has to stay over night in case any sheep are lambing.

FANTASTIC NORWAY
COASTAL CABIN
Fosen, Norway

This cabin is situated on the top of a rocky hill at the coast of Fosen, Norway. The building is carefully placed and designed in relation to the local terrain, the panoramic view, and the specific climactic conditions in the area. A variety of sheltered outdoor spaces foster a dynamic and social relationship between the cabin and the surrounding landscape.

CASEY BROWN ARCHITECTURE
BUNGEAN BEACH HOUSE
Bungan, Australia

Located on a steep slope high above Bungan Beach to the north of Sydney, this house is a series of timber pavilions situated around a sun-drenched courtyard. The site has been extensively terraced with stone walls to create level areas; zigzag stairs wind up between the pavilions.

This tree house in the state of New York serves as a room for rest and relaxation, as well as a guestroom. It is built above a wall of rocks – a place with a fantastic view over the landscape near the Hudson River. The silver-coloured tree house cabin is propped up by steel stilts; the terrace is supported by a maple tree. The visitors can reach the terrace by means of a little bridge from the top of the cliff, and the tree house by a catwalk.

American architect Roderick Romero designs and builds tree houses and landscapes around the world for clients such as Sting and Donna Karan. This tree house on a cliff belongs to American actor Val Kilmer.

1 | **BAUMRAUM**
Andreas Wenning
TREEHOUSE DJUREN
Groß Ippener, Germany

2 | SANEI HOPKINS ARCHIETCTS
PATER PAN HOUSE (FLYING PIGSTY)
Suffolk, UK

BELLEMO & CAT
COCOON
Wye River, Australia

This cocoon for weekend living is situated in a bushy coastal hamlet on the Great Ocean Road. The steepness of the site, the dramatic views, and the sometimes harsh climate resulted in an object house that, whilst protecting from the elements, is open on one side to the landscape. Basically, this is a matchbox inside an egg, a rectangle within an oval. Inside, the spaces dovetail together with the economic precision of a small boat or caravan. The lightweight monocoque structure is a hybrid of techniques appropriated from boat building and aircraft engineering.

1 | **O2 TREEEHOUSE**
Dustin Feider
O2 TREEHOUSE SEQUOIA
San Diego, USA

2 | **TREEHOUSE WORKSHOP**
Pete Nelson
LONGWOOD GARDENS 'BIRDHOUSE'
Longwood Gardens, Pennsylvania, USA

A small lookout perch at a public
arboretum in Pennsylvania.

TREEHOUSE CREATIONS
Takashi Kobayashi
NAITAIKOGEN FARM
Hokkaido, Japan

Takashi Kobayashi's TreeHouse Creations build structures on the branches of living trees worldwide. Their declared aim is to break down the feeling of separation that exists between humans and nature through art and free expression.

PATRICK DOUGHERTY

1 | **ROUNDABOUT**
Tallaght Community Art Centre,
Dublin, Ireland

2 | **JUST AROUND THE CORNER**
New Harmony, Indiana, USA

BAUMRAUM
Andreas Wenning
1 | **TREEHOUSE BACHSTELZE**
Eberschwang, Austria

BAUMRAUM
Andreas Wenning
2 | **TREEHOUSE MAGNOLIA AND PINE**
Melle, Germany

This project was built in a large private garden near Osnabrück, in northern Germany, for a family with adult children and grandchildren. The cube serves as a playground, a room for rest and relaxation, and a meeting point for business. The tree house is hidden between a group of pines but nevertheless has a view of the main house and the valley.

HELEN & HARD
BASECAMP

Prekestolen, Norway

This project by Helen & Hard consists of four different 'base camps', each for twelve to fourteen children on camping tours in the surroundings of the Prekestolen mountain lodge. Three of the base camps will open in spring 2009: the Mountain Wall, the Water Camp, and the Tree Camp. In the Mountain Wall, the children will sleep inside a steel construction attached to a steep rock wall, while at the Tree Camp, small cocoons hung around living trees will provide shelter. The Water Camp will house children in hammocks on a covered platform by a bay.

pages 131–133
WHITE ARKITEKTER
KASTRUP SØBAD
Kastrup, Denmark

The architect responsible for this seaside resort in Denmark, Frederik Petterson, has produced a structure standing on discreet legs one metre above the surface of the sea and one hundred metres out from the shore. The visitor crosses a long bridge to reach a circular installation that gradually rises up out of the sea. The installation is topped off with a trampoline at a height of five metres.

CHAPTER 04

WALK THIS WAY

NENDO

CARL-VIGGO HØLMEBAKK

ACCONCI STUDIO

Even though it is made to last, the built environment offers innumerable dynamic spaces for change and transformation. Indeed, interaction is the key to contest spatial constraints playfully within a given physical topography.

This chapter explores transit spaces, such as passageways, stairs, bridges, and mobile dwellings, that can be adapted artistically to any given restraint within the built environment. But more than just redefining existing spatial structures, these projects also transform intellectual structures, creating spaces of uncertainty and leaving bystanders to speculate about the very nature of what they are experiencing. Anish Kapoor, for example, allows a huge block of strikingly red wax to travel slowly across a white museum space, leaving dramatic marks of movement on the interior arches of the building. Gregor Schneider draws a large crowd in a one-time-only performance in which people queue for more than an hour next to the Berlin Staatsoper. They are finally let in, one by one, through a little door behind a large, moveable wall — only to find themselves back outside on the street again. Acconci Studio binds a portable park and housing unit to the blank wall of a building or sets a rowboat wedged into a circular plane of grass into the water. In the manner of Huckleberry Finn, a group of artists called the Miss Rockaway Armada constructs a fleet of rafts and journeys down the Mississippi River, stopping in towns along the way to host musical performances and vaudeville shows in the evenings. On their travels, Miss Rockaway Armada share stories about subversive and constructive ways of living.

Overcoming the confines of the prevalent, passive experience inherent to a built environment rooted in the mundane, the projects displayed here question the very concept of built-up space by soliciting dialogue and encouraging people to experience architecture as process rather than object.

NENDO

DO-HO SUH
REFLECTION
Lehmann Maupin Gallery,
New York, USA

This monumental sculpture by
Korean artist Do-Ho Suh is a full-
scale recreation of a traditional
Korean gateway in Do-Ho's childhood
home, fashioned from gossamer
aqua-blue nylon mesh.

GREGOR PASSENS
1 | **TRIUMPH**
Salinas Grandes, Jujuy, Argentina

2 | **BATTERIE**
Ludwig-Maximilian University,
Munich, Germany

3 | **BOX**
Munich, Germany

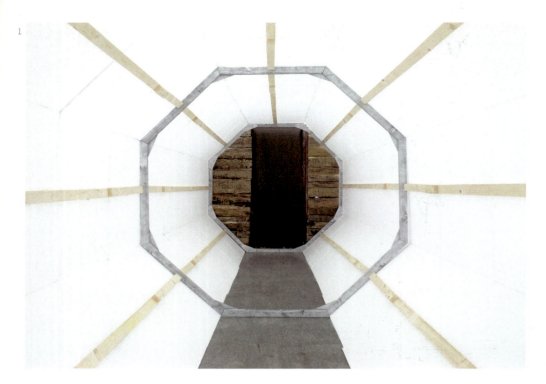

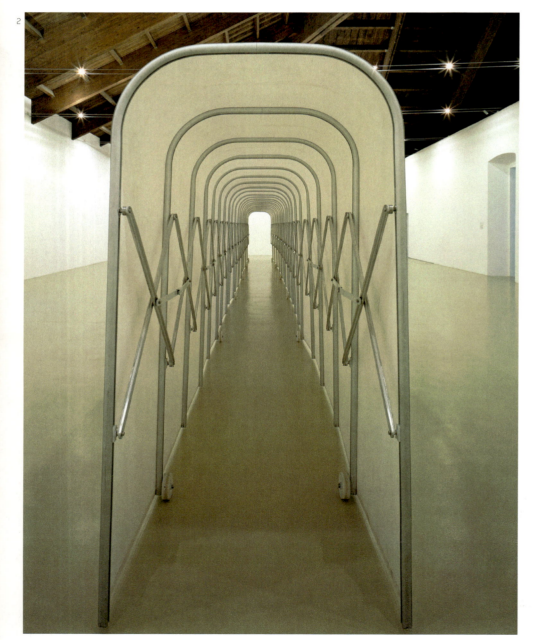

1 | **BJÖRN DAHLEM**
DEUTERIUM STADL
Vienna, Austria

The focus of Björn Dahlem's work lies in cosmology and cosmological models. With mostly simple materials like wood, Styrofoam, various light sources, and found objects, Dahlem creates sculptures that he calls 'soul landscapes' or 'mental habitats'.

2 | **GIUSEPPE GABELLONE**
UNTITLED

ANISH KAPOOR
SVAYAMBH

Musée des Beaux-arts,
Nantes, France

For the Musée des Beaux-arts de
Nantes, Anish Kapoor created a
sculpture called Svazambh – which is
a Sanskrit word meaning something
like 'shaped by its own energy'. The
work is made up of a block of red
wax put on sloping rails, elevated
about 1.5 metres above the floor of
the gallery. The block travelled slowly
through the museum, leaving dramatic marks on the arches within
its interior.

Kunstsammlung Nordrhein-Westfalen,
Düsseldorf, Germany

German artist Gregor Schneider built
a series of rooms into the existing
architecture of the museum: long
corridors and confined cells equally
reminiscent of intensive care wards
and isolation units, of protection and
confinement. Individual rooms call
to mind prison cells, interrogation
chambers, holding areas, or exercise
tracts under constant surveillance.
The title of the exhibition refer-
ences the secret and the clandestine.
'White torture', also known as 'clean
torture', entails methods that are designed to destroy a person's psyche
without leaving any external evidence.

2 | **HANS SCHABUS**
ASTRONAUT (KOMME GLEICH)
Secession, Vienna, Austria

This exhibition project by Hans Schabus
at the Secession consists of several
elements that treat the possibilities
arising from various perspectives
of 'empty space' as a sculptural
material. In the main room, Schabus
has built a true-to-scale model of
his atelier, made of cardboard and
squared timbers. It is not until one
leaves the windowless installation
that the construction and positioning
of the 'atelier' become apparent.

3 | **MICHAEL ELMGREEN &
INGAR DRAGSET
SOCIAL MOBILITY (STAIRCASE)**

This project by Michael Elmgreen
and Ingar Dragset is part of a
series called 'Powerless Structures'
that investigates the way in which
sites such as prisons, social security offices, hospitals, museums,
galleries, and parks act as means of
social control.

4 | **LES FRÈRES CHAPUISAT
INTRA MUROS N°1**
Swiss Art Awards, Basel, Switzerland

UNFOLD

with Sannah Belzer, Pieter Eeckeloo,
Christopher Paesbrugghe,
Lin Vanwayenbergh
BORDER HOUSE
Antwerp, Belgium

The design of Border House is based
on the floor plan of a nineteenth-century building. The walls parallel to the
street are collapsed, removing all the
spaces in between. What is left is a
vertical stack of walls of respective
thickness, as well as doors and window openings. The result is a collection of uncanny spaces that spatiality
only suggest – a twilight zone that
plays with notions of open-closed,
private-public, and the definition of
the place itself.

page 143
GREGOR SCHNEIDER
7:00–8:30 PM, 05.31.2007
Staatsoper Berlin, Berlin, Germany

For 7:00–8:30 PM, 05.31.2007 – a
one-time-only performance for the
Berlin Staatsoper Unter den Linden,
whose title refers to the exact time
frame of the event – Schneider drew
a large crowd to wait in line at the
entrance to the building used as a
warehouse to store the stage sets of
the State Opera's current produc-
tions. The event to take place inside,
however, remained a mystery to the
crowd waiting in line. After some de-
lay, the doors eventually opened and
the visitors were let in one by one.
Inside the building was yet another
queue, which led across a spacious

hall. After about another hour of
waiting in this second queue the visitors were once again led one by one
through a little door behind a large,
moveable wall, only to find themselves back outside on the street
again – usually leaving them puzzled
and irritated. Hinting at something
that was always about to happen
but never did left the audience with
nothing other than their own feelings
of uncertainty and absence to fill the
space of the performance.

MARCEL SCHMALGEMEIJER
15TH CINEKID

De Balie, Amsterdam, Netherlands

An entrance featuring gigantic wooden letters provided access to De Balie, a venue at Amsterdam's Cinekid Film Festival that invited children to test CD-ROMs, computer games, and websites. The three-dimensional hoarding that Schmalgemeijer created to indicate the name of the festival masked the historical façade of De Balie. Visitors entered the building through a circular hole.

MICHEL DE BROIN
HOLE
Montreal, Canada

For this project, Michel de Broin created a hole in the back of a trailer through which one can crawl inside. Open to passersby, the trailer is parked on downtown thoroughfares in the red light district.

ATELIER BOW-WOW
LIFE TUNNEL

The Hayward Gallery, London, UK

As part of the 'Psycho Buildings'
exhibition at the Hayward, the Life
Tunnel serves as a passage connecting two galleries. Its sections
transform as people progress from
crawling to walking, as if it were following a person's life.

NENDO
ILLOIHA OMOTESANDO
Tokyo, Japan

The design of this rock-climbing-inspired wall for the ILLOIHA fitness club in Tokyo uses the mismatch between a rugged outdoor sport and Tokyo's fashion district to its advantage. Instead of the usual rough and outdoorsy climbing wall, Nendo came up with the idea of using interior design elements like picture frames, mirrors, deer heads, bird cages, and flower vases to create a challenging wall with hard-to-find holds and unusual finger grips.

page 149
ALEXANDER BRODSKY
YOU PRISON
Fondazione Sandretto Re Rebaudengo, Turin, Italy

CHRISTIAN POTTGIESSER /
ARCHITECTURESPOSSIBLES
SAINT-LOUIS
Paris, France

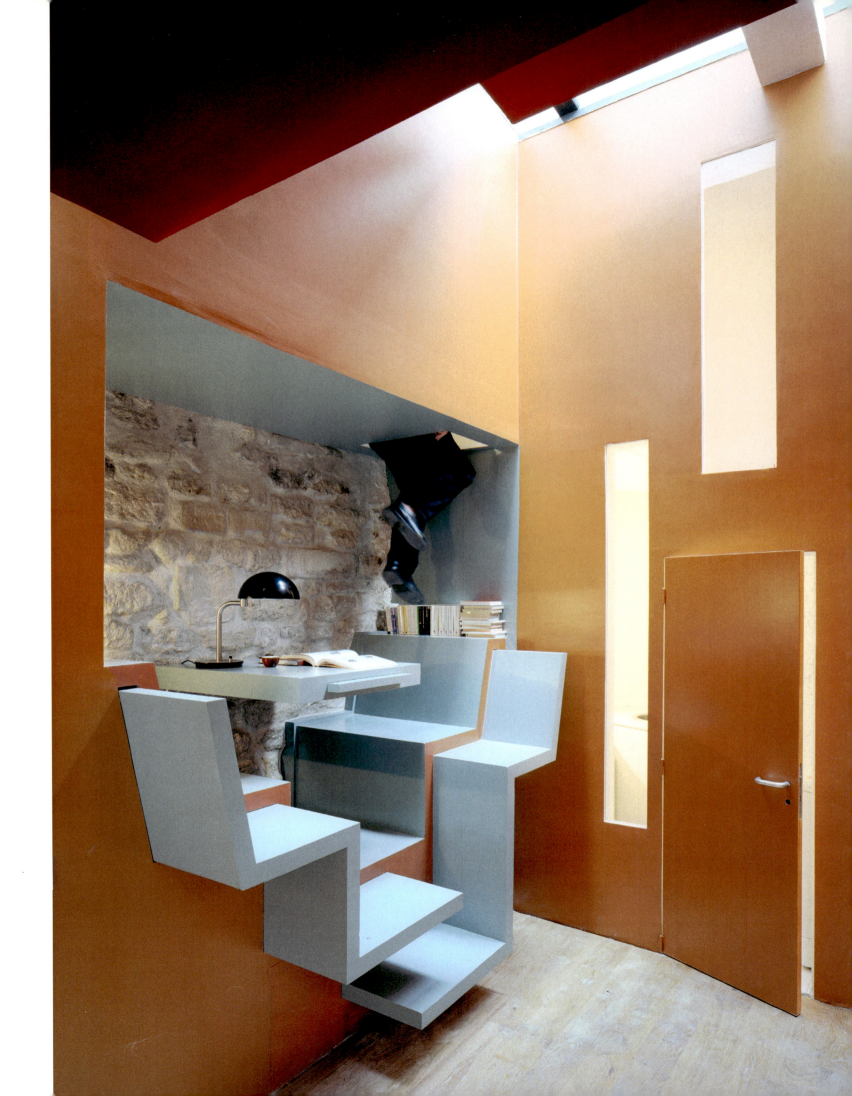

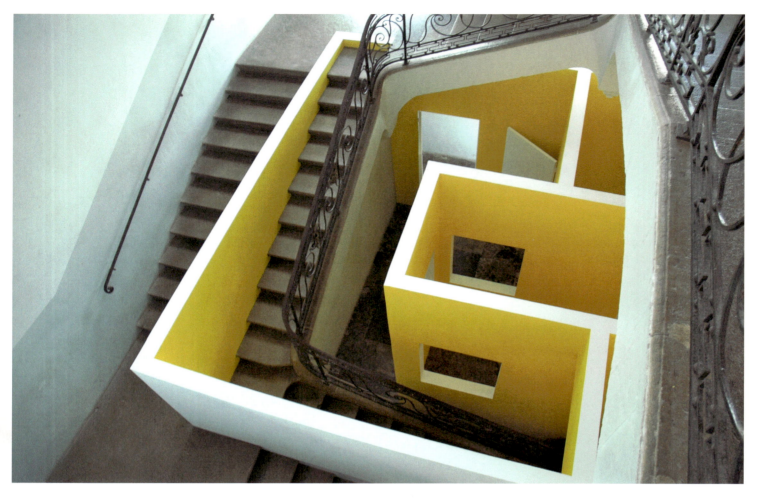

KRIJN DE KONING
WORK FOR THE ABBAYE DE CORBIGNY (YELLOW)
Corbigny, France

Temporary site-specific work, organised by the Parc Saint Léger, Centre d'art contemporain de Pougues-les-Eaux, in the main staircase of the Abbey of Corbigny.

DO-HO SUH
STAIRCASE-V
The Hayward Gallery, London, UK

1 | **GRAHAM HUDSON**
ON, OFF
Zabludowicz Collection, London, UK

For this project, Graham Hudson
occupies and responds to the main
hall of the former Methodist Chapel at
176 Prince of Wales Road, the project
space of the Zabludowicz Collection,
London. Combining a spiral structure
and a dynamic light and sound installation, On, Off exemplifies Hudson's
idiosyncratic aesthetic of do-it-
yourself amateurism, using readily
available construction materials such
as wooden pallets and scaffolding.

2 | **ACCONCI STUDIO**
PARK/HOUSE UP A BUILDING
Santiago de Compostella, Spain

This project by Vito Acconci involves
a portable park and housing, adapt-
able to the blank wall of any building.
The system consists of nine pairs
of telescoping tubes; the U-shaped
ends hook onto the parapet of the
building, and the L-shaped ends each
hold one module of the park and one
module of the house.

OSA OFFICE FOR SUBVERSIVE ARCHITECTURE
with Blueprint Magazine
POINT OF VIEW
London, UK

Londoners frustrated by the three-metre-high fence and aggressive security protecting the Olympic Park construction site in east London were given a temporary viewing platform recently by Office for Subversive Architecture. Called Point of View, the stair-like platform was created in collaboration with Blueprint magazine as a protest against the secrecy surrounding preparations for the 2012 Olympics, but was removed by security guards after two days.

MICHAEL BEUTLER
YELLOW ESCALATOR
4th Berlin Biennial, Germany

1 | **BUREAU DES MÉSARCHITECTURES**
Didier Fiuza Faustino
STAIRWAY TO HEAVEN
Castelo Branco, Portugal

The Stairway to Heaven project plays on the ambiguity of public and private spaces: it offers a public space for individual use while utilising the figure of the collective housing stairway, which is a public space within a private property.

GIUSEPPE GABELLONE
2 | **PERIODO**
3 | **UNTITLED**

page 157
HENRY KROKATSIS
AMBO
Sudeley Castle, Gloucestershire, UK

Henry Krokatsis coils a white gothic pulpit around an old tree flecked with ivy and studded with fungi for 'The Artist's Playground', an annual open-air exhibition at Sudeley Castle.

1 | FELD72
WOLKON
Paasdorf, Austria

Paasdorf is a small village in Lower Austria. The task of feld72 was to position 'Kulturlandschaft Paasdorf' – an art project that has developed over a period of ten years and is known far beyond the borders of Austria – by means of a symbol on the newly designed village square. The bus stop – the Wolkon – functions as a landmark and information compass. The accessible roof is a lounge, DJ pulpit, speaker's corner, and open-air gallery.

2 | A12
DEEP GARDEN
Venice, Italy

The open-air room built in front of the gardens of the Biennale takes on the force of nature and opposes it, offering an isolated place to enjoy the silence and to submerge oneself in a surreal space. In a city like Venice, where the unique feature of the town is its immersion in the lagoon, this temporary garden reflects the surrounding landscape and becomes a symbol of the flow of energy through which man constructs new experiences in seemingly inconceivable places.

3 | **ATMOS**
Alex Haw
W/S/P/T
Hong Kong/Guangzhou, China

W/S/P/T is an abbreviation for Work/Space/Ply/Time. British architect Alex Haw has designed it as a movable pavilion. More than an installation set, it is a huge building that can be separated or assembled in a short time.

4 | **PEZO VON ELLRICHSHAUSEN**
120 DOORS
Concepcion, Chile

Exploring the points of transmission or friction between one place and another, this work is a uniform spatial structure of steel tubes and 120 standard wooden doors. Seen from the outside, the exterior perimeter is a compact horizontal block. The interior space is closed laterally and opens to the sky and the ground.

GREGOR SCHNEIDER
BONDI BEACH / 21 BEACH CELLS
Sydney, Australia

This site-specific installation for the
Kaldro Art Projects at Sydney's Bondi
Beach is a free-standing work consisting of twenty-one identical cells,
constructed of typical Australian
fencing. Each cell contains amenities
for visitors, such as an air mattress,
beach umbrella, and garbage bag.

**OSA OFFICE FOR SUBVERSIVE
ARCHITECTURE**
with Thomas Deyle & KunstWerk Köln
ANWOHNERPARK (RESIDENT'S PARK)
Cologne, Germany

EBERHARD BOSSLET
1 | **SAARSTERN 01/06**
Stadtgalerie Saarbrücken, Germany

The instant sculpture series Circles
for public space consists of industrial units that are connected,
contrary to their conventional use,
to new mega-structures.

2 | **AKQUISITION 33/77**
Garden Centre Dresden

1 | **CARVE**
WALL-HOLLA
Purmerend, Netherlands

This vertical urban play-structure combines several functions that appeal to different age groups. It is a crawl-through maze, a climbing wall, and a lounge object. It may function as a ball-catcher at the end of a football field. Because of its modular system, the Wall-holla can be made in different sizes with various combinations. It can even be extended with a football goal, with slides, or with fireman poles.

2 | **LAGOMBRA**
Anders Jakobsen
BICYCLE ROLLERCOASTER
Eindhoven, Netherlands

The Swedish artist and designer Anders Jakobsen, also known as Lagombra, has created a bicycle rollercoaster for the MU Art Foundation in Eindhoven, the Netherlands, to coincide with the designhuis exhibition 'The Dutch Bicycle'. Constructed of raw wood and scaffolding, and fabricated with little more than a chainsaw, the installation resembles an undulating series of toppled dominoes.

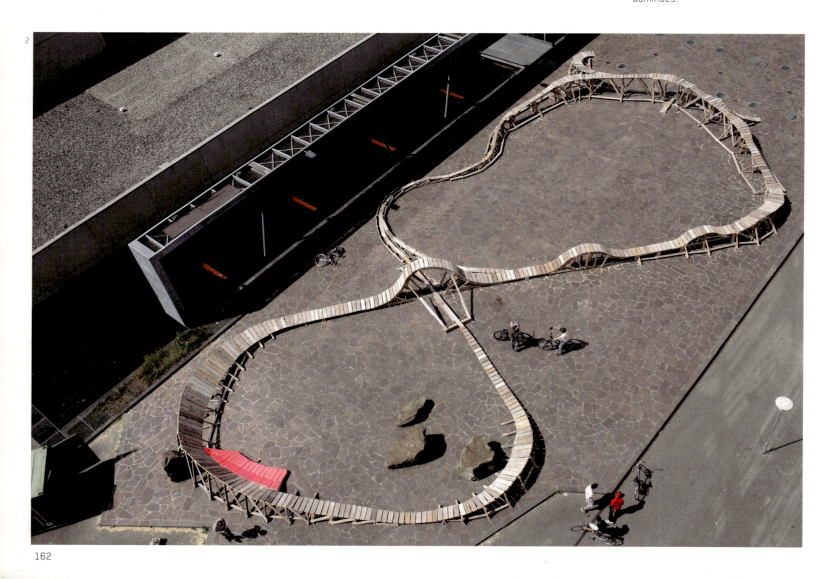

KAI SCHIEMENZ
3 | **TOWER TO NOWHERE**
Federal Foreign Office, Berlin,
Germany

This sculpture consists of a seven-
metre-high wooden stairway that
was constructed in the atrium of
the Federal Foreign Office. It loops
around itself in such a way that
people ascending it from various
sides come together and mirror
each other.

KAI SCHIEMENZ
4 | **THE EMPTY DWELLING, THE VAIN
TOWER AND THE MAD COLONIST**
Skulpturenpark, Berlin, Germany

This sculpture, made from roof bat-
tens and plywood, was part of the
exhibition 'Speculation' organised by
Skulpturenpark Berlin. The three-part
structure – a stairway, platform, and
double-spiralled tower – was situated
in an inner-city wasteland space
that had formerly been part of the
no-man's-land behind the Berlin Wall
and that remains undeveloped today.

KAI SCHIEMENZ
5 | **TOTAL THEATRE – COMMUNUAL
THEATRE**
Riga, Latvia

This work came about in relation to the idea of the Theatre of
Memory described in 1550 by the
Renaissance scholar Giulio Camillo.
In this theatre, which reverses the
normal perspective of such buildings,
the spectator stands at the centre
and looks into the auditorium, which
represents the world.

HEATHERWICK STUDIO
ROLLING BRIDGE
London, UK

ACCONCI STUDIO
MUR ISALND
Graz, Austria

A twist in the river, a node in the river, a circulation-route in the river. The node is an island; it is a dome that twists into a bowl that twists into a dome. Vito Acconci's Mur Island project functions as a café and restaurant.

The entrance canopy twists down to create lounge seating around the dome. Curved triangular tables and stools are movable; they are joined together for different-sized groups of people. The rubber edge of the terrace above twists down to form multiple bar counters at different heights. Up on the terrace, guests sit under a waterfall formed by water pouring down the shell of the dome.

GERMÁN DEL SOL
GEOMETRIC HOT SPRINGS
Villarica National Park, Chile

In his Geometric Hot Springs, Germán del Sol diverted a natural source of hot water with colourful architecture and green roofs. The Geometric Hot Springs are located in the middle of native forests of Villarrica National Park. For pleasurable bathing in the midst of nature, seventeen pools were carved along 450 metres, with red wooden paths and a stepless ramp that leads visitors to the pools and lets them walk through the project to choose a pool in which to bathe.

CARL-VIGGO HØLMEBAKK
SOHLBERGPLASSEN VIEWPOINT
Atnasjø, Stor-Elvdal, Norway

HAAS & HAHN
FAVELA PAINTING
Vila Cruzeiro, Rio de Janeiro

Haas & Hahn are working on large murals in Vila Cruzeiro, a notorious Rio slum tormented by the ongoing war between the local drug gang and the police. This mural, called Rio Cruzeiro, depicts a Japanese-style river flowing through the favela, complete with carp swimming upstream. The painting spans approximately 2000 square metres and was created together with local youth. Such community-driven interventions draw positive media attention to these neighbourhoods and their inhabitants, improving the otherwise exclusively negative image projected by the media. At the same time, the project instils a sense of pride and self-esteem among local residents.

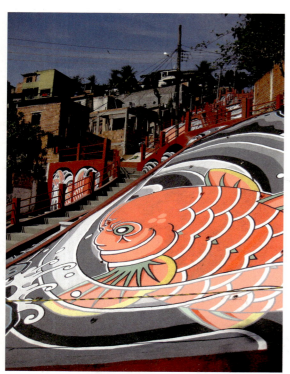

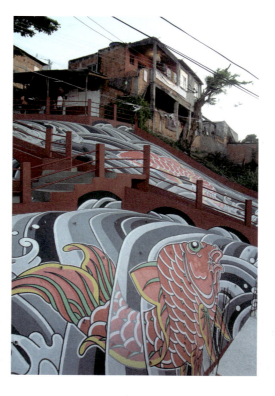

INTERBREEDING FIELD
JELLO MAZE

National Taiwan Museum of Fine Arts,
Taichung, Taiwan / Capital Plaza of
R.O.C., Taipei, Taiwan

A group of young architectural
talents led by Liu Li-Huang were
commissioned by the National
Taiwan Museum of Fine Arts to create a square Jello Maze installation
in front of the Presidential Office in
celebration of the Lunar New Year.
A total of 7200 large, translucent
plastic kegs were joined to form a
zigzagging serpentine wall, which
was illuminated from within.

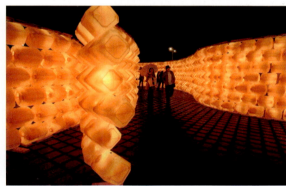

**ANNA GALTAROSSA &
DANIEL GONZÁLEZ
CHILI MOON TOWN TOUR**
Lake at Chapultepec Park, Mexico City

This floating town was born on the
waters of Chapultepec Lake in Mexico
City. Chili Moon Town Tour is a utopian
floating city of dreams that knows no
boundaries. It is born as a free city
without frontiers. It does not force its
inhabitants to migrate, but migrates
itself. It is a metropolis with futuristic
handmade skyscrapers, a place that
overcomes stressful traffic, ethnical
differences, beliefs, and ideologies.

page 174

MISS ROCKAWAY ARMADA
FLOTILLA
Missippi River, USA

The Miss Rockaway Armada is a group of approximately thirty performers and artists from all over the United States who constructed a flotilla of rafts that will float down the Mississippi River. Miss Rockaway Armada will stop in towns along the way, hosting musical performances and vaudeville variety-theatre in the evenings, along with workshops and skill-sharing centred around arts and environmental issues during the day. During their travels, Miss Rockaway Armada intend to share stories and solicit dialogue centred on subversive and constructive ways of living.

page 175

RAUMLABORBERLIN
CAPE FEAR
Mannheim, Germany

On a central square in the city of Mannheim, a submarine was built within ten days from pieces of old wood, junk, and scrap-metal plates. raumlabor berlin then set out on a voyage along the Neckar and Rhine to the city of Ludwigshafen. A crew of ten people was cast to navigate the vessel on the difficult passages, participate in the building of the boat, and pull the boat to the river. After it arrived safely at its destination, it was pulled to and taken into custody by the public art gallery of Ludwigshafen.

1 | SEBASTIAN DENZ
UNTITLED

2 | N55, ARTIST GROUP
WALKING HOUSE
Copenhagen, Denmark

Walking House is a modular dwelling system that enables people to live a peaceful, nomadic life while moving slowly through the landscape or cityscape with minimal impact on the environment.

It collects energy from its surroundings using solar cells and small windmills. There is a system for collecting rainwater and a system for solar-heated hot water. A composting toilet system allows for disposal of sewage produced by the inhabitants.

STEPHAN KÖPERL, SYLVIA WINKLER,
MARWA ZAKARIA
3RABIET ELSA3ADA
Cairo, Egypt

'3rabiet elsa3ada', the car of happi-
ness, was designed to collect state-
ments that start with 'I am happy
because...' in various districts of
Cairo. The collaborative work by
Sylvia Winkler, Stephan Köperl, and
Marwa Zakaria was organised by
the Goethe Institute of Cairo.

1 | DENIS OUDENDIJK & ROSA HAGEN
CARABANA ROSA
Nantes, France

pages 178 / 2, 179

EDOUARD SAUTAI
PIÈCE DÉTACHÉE
Blanc-Mesnil, France

The sculpture and utopian architecture project Pièce détachée is a removable extension of a flat in Iwona Buczkowska's residency complex. The project took place during the Art Grandeur Nature Biennial 2008.

CHAPTER 05

JUST LOSE IT

RAUMLABORBERLIN

ANNA GALTAROSSA & DANIEL GONZÁLEZ

We live in a world of planned obsolescence, in which everything gets thrown away and very few products marketed to consumers are made to last. Ours is a disposable society, strongly influenced by consumerism and based on over-consumption.

With this in mind, the chapter Just Lose It provides not only an inspiring look at the creative potential of recycling left-over and waste construction materials, but also at the loss of control and break-down of form in ever-eclectic structures. Everything from doors, windows, tyres, and cars to cardboard buildings and vast miniature cities made of lost and salvaged goods can be found here. The work of the Dutch architecture / art group Refunc, led by Jan Korbes and Denis Oudendijk, is exemplary of this extraordinary creativity in reusing discarded objects. For a Lithuanian refrigerator recycling company, for example, they took hundreds of fridges and used them to build a huge, partly illuminated wall, including windows and a balcony, creating a positive visual connection between the factory and the nearby highway. The Maison Millegomme, a garden house with office and storage space, was designed and built using materials from a gently dismantled, old garden house, as well as local waste materials such as car tyres and insulated glass. Other notable examples are SALZIG Design's Temple of Trash, made of 100 tonnes of pressed PET bottles; Gonzales's over-the-top installations; or Ai Weiwei's documenta 12 installation called Template, made of worn wooden doors and windows from destroyed Chinese temples – a work demolished by gusts of wind during the opening days of the international art exhibition in Kassel, Germany. Weiwei subsequently declared the work to be even more beautiful than before, teaching us that coincidence, and a possible loss of control, should always be included in the overall calculation. It may very well be that a mistake leads the way to an ideal solution.

All works in this chapter vividly illustrate that an aesthetic of the unfinished and the makeshift can reshape our notions of useful and useable space.

AI WEIWEI

PIET HEIN EEK
KRÖLLER–MÖLLER TICKET HOUSE
Otterlo, Netherlands

The group of creative minds around Dutch artist and designer Peit Hein Eek succeeds in making unique products of worthless and disposable material, ranging from furniture and interior design to architecture. The combination of uncommon materials and also uncommon, but simple methods of working has become the thread connecting their oeuvre.

KEES VAN DER HOEVEN
FLOWERPOT HOUSE
Wassenaar, Netherlands

In Wassenaar, Kees van der Hoeven – Architect, former president of the Royal Institute of Dutch Architects BNA and initiator of Architectenwerk, has transformed an old shipping container into his private studio. Three façades are clad with flowerpots. By using the conical shape of one-screw-fixed pots, the construction keeps the other, reversed ones, in place.

1 | FELIX JERUSALEM
STRAW HOUSE
Eschenz, Switzerland

The Staw House in Switzerland was designed by architect Felix Jerusalem using compressed straw bale. The house is a modern, prefab take on straw-bale construction, employing a prefabricated, compressed straw-bale kit of parts to assemble the house in wall-sized pieces. The exterior is clad with translucent composite sheeting material, which protects the straw-bale prefab units from the elements.

2 | PIET HEIN EEK
GARDENHOUSE TEAROOM
Groningen, Netherlands

UNIVERSITY OF SHEFFIELD / SCHOOL OF ARCHITECTURE
SPACE OF WASTE
Sheffield, UK

Space of Waste's objective was to create something beautiful out of what most people would perceive as rubbish. Employing materials exclusively sourced from www.whywaste. org.uk – a free materials exchange for waste from the construction industries – the project sought to prove that such material could be used to build structurally sound and aesthetically pleasing buildings, and serve as a demountable exhibition space to be toured around the UK in order to increase public awareness of diverting waste material from landfill.

KÖBBERLING KALTWASSER
WERDPLATZPALAIS
Werdplatz, Zurich

1 | KÖBBERLING KALTWASSER
AMPHIS
Wysing Arts Centre, Cambridge,
England

With the aid of volunteers and in-
trigued onlookers, Folke Köbberling
and Martin Kaltwasser have been
building a giant amphitheatre out of
junk. As a study in patchwork construction, it is a mysterious space of
chambers fabricated by borrowers.

2 | CONSTRUCTLAB
LE MANABLE
Argentan, France

In 2006 the popular French phi-
losopher Michel Onfray founded a
rather unconventional free evening
university in Normandy, France.
Classes included cooking courses in
collaboration with a shared garden
project. With the initial support
of French architect and curator
Patrick Bouchain, constructLab built
a place of pleasure and recreation
for the gardeners and the members
of the university in a participative
process. The architects lived on-
site for three months of building in
order to seek reusable materials.
They had to be strongly reactive and
rethink the project according to the
proposed materials.

REFUNC.NL
Denis Oudendijk and Jan Körbes

Garbage architecture is providing a second life for objects that are found or thrown-away. Refunc.nl operate on the borders of architecture, art, and design and create new products from old materials. The origins of the designs are found in the objects themselves, by listening to their own composition, history, or local and social context.

1 | **ADD-ON 2**
New Crossroads, Capetown, South Africa

Working together and exchanging experiences with locals in the township of New Crossroads, Capetown, Refunc.nl created a series of objects made from old car tyres. These range from a playground in the local church yard and extensions of community houses to numerous add-on structures in the community.

REFUNC.NL
2 | **MAISONGOMME**
The Hague, Netherlands

This garden house with office and storage function has been designed on-site and built with materials from the gently demolished old garden house and other local waste materials, such as car tyres and insulation glass.

REFUNC.NL
3 | **CHAINRIDERS**
Cascoland Drill Hall, Johannesburg, South Africa

This project evolved during the intercultural and interdisciplinary Cascoland Art Festival in the centre of Johannesburg.The absence of playgrounds motivated the artists to install thirty swings made of recovered car tyres on the façade arches of an old unused movie theatre.

REFUNC.NL
4 | REQUIEM LT
Vilnius, Lithuania

This chapel-like installation made of crashed cars serves to encourage safer driving habits in Lithuania.

5 | THE FINCHMOB, REBAR & CMG LANDSCAPE
PANHANDLE BANDSHELL
San Francisco, USA

The Panhandle Bandshell is a full-scale performance stage constructed almost entirely out of reclaimed and repurposed materials, including sixty-five automobile hoods, hundreds of computer circuit boards, 3000 plastic water bottles, French doors, reclaimed wood, and recycled structural steel. As a fully modular structure, it can be easily dismantled, moved, and re-assembled anywhere. In the summer of 2007, it was installed in San Francisco's Golden Gate Park, where it was open for both impromptu and scheduled performances.

1 | STORTPLAATS VAN DROMEN
EXPOSITION SPACE
Utrecht, Netherlands

Exposition Space is built in a former
distribution centre with the simple
change of building one wall out of reused double-glazed doors. The doors
were not cut, and thus they can be
reused when demounted.

2 | CHIHARU SHIOTA
INSIDE/OUTSIDE
Goff+Rosenthal Berlin, Germany

This site-specific and room-encompassing installation by Japanese artist
Chiharu Shiota consists of a towering
structure of windows, which stands
like the remnant of a construction
that has been left behind.

page 189
THOMAS RENTMEISTER
NEARLY 100 FRIDGES IN A CORNER
Greenaway Art Gallery (GAG Projects),
Adelaide, Australia

For this monumental installation
made of garbage at the Adelaide
Festival of Arts, German artist
Thomas Rentmeist piled nearly 100
refrigerators on top of each other,
reminiscent of a landscape or ancient ruin.

REFUNC.NL
Denis Oudendijk and Jan Körbes
RETURN OF THE FRIDGES
Vilnius, Lithuania

This is a visual barrier with light signing and views to the landscape between a refrigerator recycling company and the highway. It is made of 700 reused refrigerators and numerous coloured tubular lamps. The idea was to provide the factory with a positive visual connection with the Lithuanian landscape and the highway.

1 | WINTER / HÖRBELT
KASTENHAUS 1066.13
Padova, Italy

While in the early stages of their 'Cratehouse serial', Winter and Hoerbelt worked with used plastic crates from everywhere in the world as building material. For Kastenhaus 1066.13 the artists employed interesting light effects and UV protection.

2 | ONIX
CRATE HOUSE
Barevel, Netherlands

This structure is made of potato boxes in a small farming town in the Netherlands and is the reaction to the possible withdrawal of state subsidies for growing starch potatoes in this area of the country in 2006. The potato boxes represent the area's past as well as its expectations for the future. Local youth helped to build the structure, giving the boxes a new use.

AMENITY SPACE
with No Fixed Abode &
WhyWaste.org.UK
ONE NIGHT HOUSE
Berlin, Germany

One Night House was a collaborative
project centred around the design
and construction of a one night
house on Alexanderplatz, Berlin, as
part of the New Life Berlin festival.
The project explored the folk law
of the one night house: it is said
that if someone can build a house in
one night without any disturbances
and have smoke rising from the
chimney by dawn, then the plot that
the house stands on will be beholden
to the builder. Within only a couple
of hours, the finished house was
standing with smoke rising from the
chimney. Around fifty participants
contributed to its construction, forming a productive, positive, and eager
community of interested parties.

2 | **FRANZ HÖFNER, HARRY SACHS,
MICHAEL BOEHLER &
MARKUS LOHMANN
DAS BESCHÄFT**
Kunstverein Harburg, Germany

This accessible three-storey installation made from industrial leftovers,
such as pallets and packaging material, even has a model railroad running through it on a luggage belt.

SALZIG DESIGN
TEMPLE OF TRASH
Rotterdam, Netherlands

At Heijplaat, an old district of Rotterdam, during the folly festival Follydock 2007, the Salzig Design team created the Temple of Trash. The construction consisted of 100 bales of pressed PET bottles from a nearby recycling company.

AI WEIWEI
TEMPLATE
documenta 12, Kassel, Germany

This large structure made of worn wooden doors and windows from destroyed Ming and Qing Dynasty Chinese temples by Chinese celebrity artist Ai Weiwei was demolished by a gust of wind during documenta 12. The artist, however, proclaimed his enthusiasm for the mishap, declaring it to be more beautiful than before.

page 195
DORIS SALCEDO
INSTALLATION FOR 8TH
INTERNATIONAL ISTANBUL BIENNIAL
Istanbul, Turkey

This built explosion was designed
for a festival centre at the 2008
Steirischer Herbst Festival in Graz.

1 | **SITU STUDIO**
SOLAR PAVILION 2
Stuyvesant Cove Park, New York, NY

Solar Pavilion 2, Situ Studio's second pavilion in a series of three has been constructed four times, each time on a different site by different participants and with unique programmatic requirements. The pavilion relies on properties of self-organisation found in natural systems to create a lightweight structure that is easily constructed using local assembly rules and no definitive plan, allowing for multiple spatial configurations. The first deployment took place on the east side of Manhattan at Stuyvesant Cove Park in the summer of 2007. It accommodated a bar, a food counter, and a wind-power signup drive.

2 | **GELITIN**
STELLUNGSWECHSEL 500
Konsthall Malmö, Sweden

HACKENBROICH ARCHITEKTEN
THE TRAFFIC OF CLOUDS
Program Gallery, Berlin, Germany

The Traffic of Clouds is a large-scale, site-specific installation developed by Hackenbroich Architekten in collaboration with Jan Christensen. The logic of weaving and constant movement pervades both the built form and the wall painting. The tension in the wood fibres of the interwoven boards forms sturdy walls of lace, redefining both the visual effect and the intended use of the wooden boards.

ECOLOGICSTUDIO
with Architectural Association,
Columbia University, and
Politecnico di Torino
BIODEGRADING PAVILLION
Turin, Italy

This biodegrading pavilion was designed in Turin during the prototyping by City Design Studio, a collaborative workshop organised by the Torino World Design Capital 2008, the Architectural Association, the Graduate School of Architecture, Planning and Preservation at Columbia University, and the Polytechnic of Turin within the context of the summer school Designing Connected Places.

It is the result of an intensive two-week collaborative project directed by Claudia Pasquero and Marco Poletto [Architectural Association / ecoLogicStudio] with Caterina Tiazzoldi [Columbia University] and Cesare Griffa [Politecnico di Torino] with thirty-five international students and the support of Denaldi Legnami.

HEW LOCKE
HEMMED IN TWO
Luckman Fine Arts Complex,
California State University, USA

Hew Locke's installation Hemmed In
Two, is partly boat, partly a package,
and partly a personal reflection on
the global commodification of culture
and its history. The piece grew
organically and is reconfigured for
each new venue.

HEW LOCKE
CARDBOARD PALACE
Chisenhale Gallery, London, UK

This installation was a vast architectural construction first exhibited during the celebrations commemorating the Golden Jubilee of Queen Elizabeth II. Visitors moved through a series of spaces akin to grottoes or state rooms and filled with images of the British Royal Family. The Cardboard Palace is a massive drawing that started with flat pieces of cardboard, which were then cut, painted, drawn, folded, bent, and glued together to become a sculpture.

**FERNANDO AND HUMBERTO
CAMPANA
OCA INSTALLATION**

Vitra Design Museum, Weil am Rhein,
Germany

This installation made of straw by the
Campana Brothers for the 'My Home'
exhibition at Vitra Design Museum is
exemplary for the way in which the
two Brazilian designers effortlessly
cross boundaries in design, sculpture, and art to create new hybrid
and sustainable forms.

TOBIAS PUTRIH
VENETIAN, ATMOSPHERIC
Venice, Italy

This installation by Tobias Purith was originally conceived for the Slovenian Pavilion on the Island of San Servolo at the 52nd Venice Biennial.

SUPERBLUE DESIGN
1 | HONEYCOMB RETREAT
London, UK

This retreat by Superblue Design uses honeycomb panels on three sides and is set within a green oak deck.

2 | THE POTTING SHED
London, UK

The Potting Shed creates a space for people to shelter and potter within their own gardens. Using the Honeycomb Fence panel, the shed allows a surface where plants can be planted, seeded, and stored.

JOLIAN & LUFT
SIMPLY-CITY
Lund, Sweden

This project arose as a collaboration between the Swedish landscape architect Louise Andersson and artist/designer Jonas Liverod for the exhibition 'Capital', curated by Caroline Lund.

page 205 / 1
ANARCHITECT LTD
BARRIO NORTH
London, UK

The interior of Barrio North, a bar by London architects Anarchitect, features a transformed caravan. The caravan has been modified to create seating with artwork displayed in light boxes where the windows used to be.

page 205 / 2
JOE COLEMAN
THE ODDITORIUM
KW Institute for Contemporary Art, Berlin, Germany

American artist Joe Coleman paints, draws, performs, and collects. His obsessive work includes panel paintings, comic strips, performances, and a total installation – all related to each other in a complex web of mutual referencing. In 2007, KW Berlin had a majestic showing of Coleman's most compelling and visceral pieces, including this room-encompassing installation.

PETER CALLESEN
FLOATING CASTLE
Hamburg, Germany

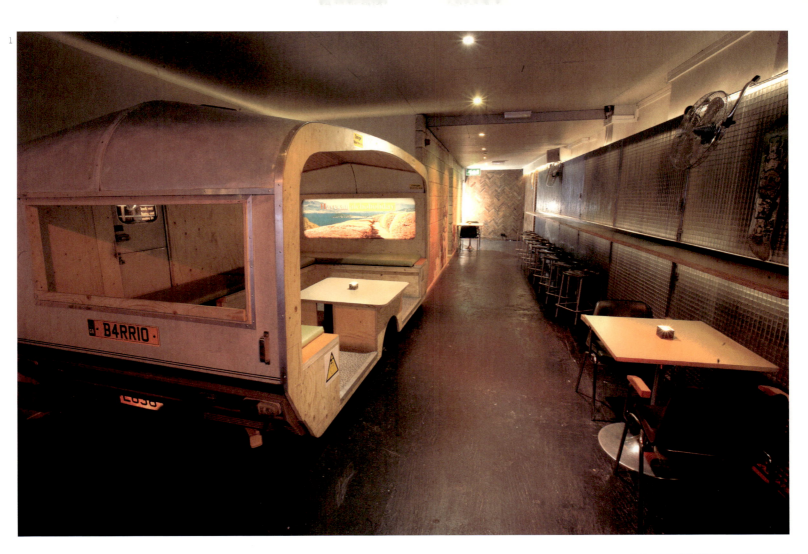

page 206
ROB VOERMAN
ANNEX # 4
Variable locations

This sculpture was initially commissioned as a solo exhibition for
Rob Voerman at the Architectural
Association in London in 2006. The
work can be entered by visitors
through the door of the upside-
down car.

page 207
ROB VOERMAN
TARNUNG # 2
BodhiBerlin, Berlin, Germany

This sculpture was created for the
exhibition 'Urban Spiel' at BodhiBerlin,
curated by Shaheen Merali. Inside
the sculpture, an odd composition of
fragments of various religious music
is played very softly on the radio.

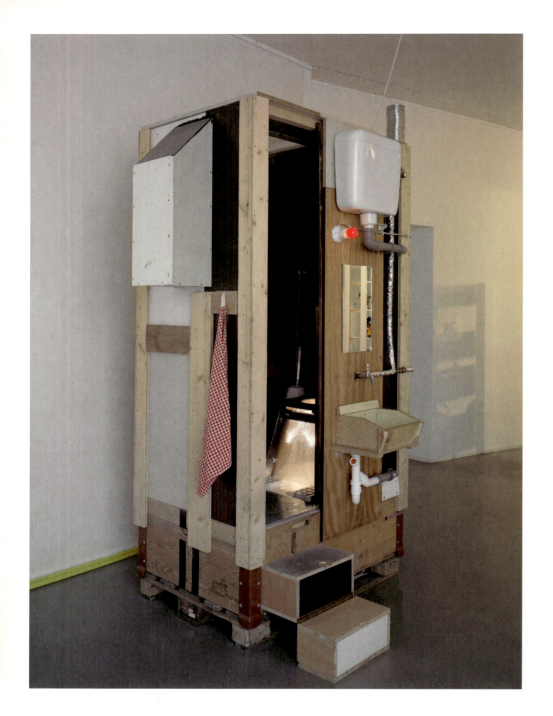

GELITIN
LOCUS FOCUS
La Louvre – Paris, Musée d'Art moderne
de la Ville de Paris

This installation by the Austrian
artist collective Gelitin consists of a
toilet with an integrated four-mirror
system and a pair of binoculars. When
sitting down, visitors can experience
and see their own behind up close
through the binoculars.

JONAS LIVERÖD
IDIOT ISLAND
Ystad Museum of Art, Ystad, Sweden

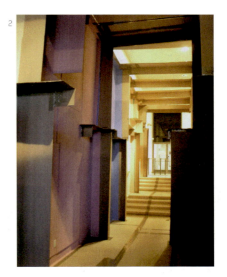

CARLOS BUNGA

1 | INSTALLATION
Porto, Portugal

Portuguese artist Carlos Bunga uses materials such as pressed cardboard, paint, and wrapping tape to build rooms that extrude like outgrowths stuck onto existing constructions or architectures.

2 | INSTALLATION
San Diego Museum of Art, California, USA

3 | KURSAAL PROJECT
Manifest 05, San Sebastián, Spain

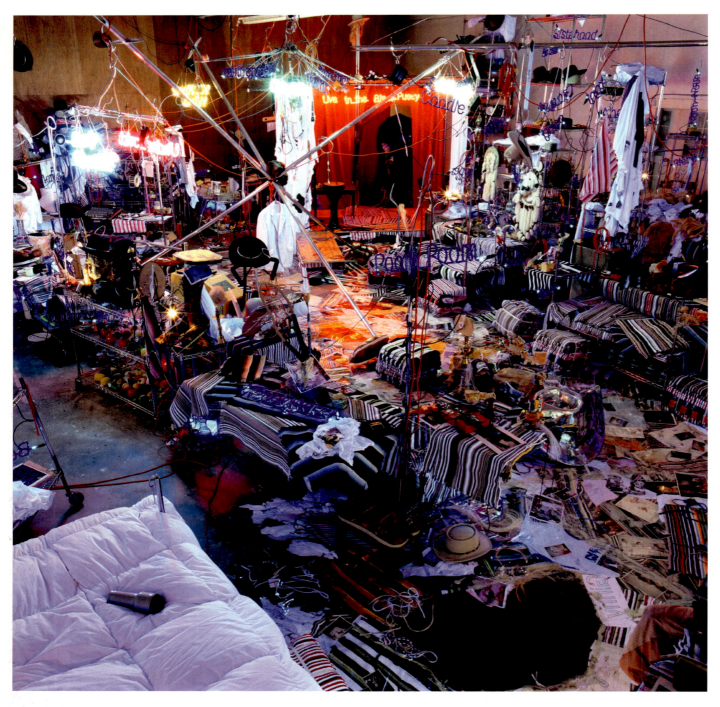

page 210

JASON RHOADES
BLACK PUSSY

This installation by American artist
Jason Rhoades, who passed away
in 2006, is one of the last works he
conceived and was completed shortly
before his death. Sprawling over
roughly 3000 square feet, the work
presents itself as a large installation,
dominated by an empty stage bearing
a neon sign that reads 'Live in the
Black Pussy.' The work also features
185 neon pussy word signs, as part
of the artist's ongoing project of
creating a cross-cultural compendium
of synonyms for female genitalia.
Large storage racks are covered with
myriad objects, including hundreds of
Egyptian Hookah pipes from a seized
shipping container, Native American
fetishes, beaver-felt cowboy hats,
Chinese Scholar stones, Venetian
glass vegetables, colourful cloth rugs,
and more.

MICHAEL BEUTLER
PORTIKUS CASTLE
Portikus, Frankfurt / Main, Germany

For his sculptural installation at
Portikus, Beutler takes advantage
of the full height of the exhibition space. Using metal grids clad
in transparent paper and woven
together into surfaces, the artist
builds a room-filling sculpture.

ELTONO & NURIA MORA
EIGENKONSTRUKTION

'Urban Grassroots' exhibition,
Berlin, Germany

For the 'Urban Grassroots' exhibition
curated by Artitude e.V., the Madrid
artists Eltono & Nuria Mora created
this favela-like structure out of
cardboard and wooden boxes.

ETIENNE BOULANGER
PLUG-IN BERLIN
Berlin, Germany

Because of its conversion, destruction, and desertion, the city provides Etienne Boulanger with moving surroundings for his artistic experiments. His work is not set in a process of representation or production of objects; first and foremost, it is a political and social stance in our urban environment. The spaces he locates, surrounds, and takes over have no status and become the medium for interventions that interfere but cause only very slight alterations to the architecture. They are makeshift shelters that enable the artist to spend the night. The work carried out in 2001 and 2002 was aimed primarily at being a nomadic experiment in an urban environment. Micro-spaces that had been left vacant following Berlin's almost total renovation became locales with the potential to be occupied and turned into living spaces.

ETIENNE BOULANGER

1 | PLUG-IN BERLIN, SHELTER #10,
ALEXANDERPLATZ

2 | PLUG-IN BERLIN, SHELTER #13,
JOACHIMSTRASSE

3 | PLUG-IN BERLIN, SHELTER #04,
MONBIJOUBRÜCKE

DANIELA BRAHM

1 | THE NEW TOWN
Zamosc, Poland

The work The New Town imitates the signs seen on fences around construction sites and announces a fictitious building project. The New Town does not present a concrete plan, however, but rather anonymously occupies a position that harks back to the formal vocabulary of post-war modernism and participatory models of the city.

2 | RECYCLING UTOPIA #1
Potsdam, Germany

Recycling Utopia in the city of Potsdam not far from Berlin is the follow-up project to The New Town. Announcing the original building project, the component parts of the installation have been downgraded to simple building materials, and the recycled installation is now located in a gloomy corner of a 1970s tower block.

UNIVERSITY OF KASSEL
Philipp Oswalt, Kilian Enders & Oliver Vogt
OPEN VILLAGE
Kassel, Germany

Under the direction of Prof. Philipp Oswalt and Kilian Enders from the Department of Architecture Theory and Design and of Prof. Oliver Vogt from the Department of Industrial Design, a temporary city was installed by students for the visitors of the documenta 12 exhibition.

3 | Janine Gerland, Klaus Scholl
MOCTAGON

4 | Eva Bender, Lena Plake
THE KNOT

5 | Jonathan Keune, David Roth
LIVINGBOWL

LARS Ø RAMBERG
LIBERTÉ
La Biennale di Venezia,
The Nordic Pavilion, Venice, Italy

When Jacques Chirac was mayor of
Paris, he challenged the French company JCDecaux to design unisex public
toilets, reflecting on and fulfilling the
French ideal of individual rights in
a democratic society. In 1979 Jean
Claude Decaux presented the very
first self-cleaning toilets in the world.
In 2003, Rambergs proposed his
project Liberté, which consisted of a
version of three of the original toilets
from 1979 taken from the streets of
Paris, refurbished, and painted in red,
white, and blue, which are the colours
of the national flags of Norway,
France, and the United States. The
enclosures carry the inscriptions
'liberté', 'egalité', 'fraternité' and
three different radio programmes
broadcast historical speeches inside.
Charles de Gaulle, King Haakon VII and
Franklin D. Roosevelt are accompanied by the national hymns of Norway,
France, and the USA.

ALLAN WEXLER
THE NEW YORK VOTER
REGISTRATION CENTER
New York City, USA

The National Voter Registration
Center reached out to unregis-
tered college students to encourage their participation in the 2008
presidential election. Folded into
a car and unfurled in minutes on
site, the Registration Center was
staffed by student volunteers. The
centre is constructed from layers of
white peg board that sandwich the
American flag.

1 | **GREGOR PASSENS**
HOLIDAY ON ICE
Ebrach, Germany

This temporary ice-skating rink in the courtyard of a juvenile prison in Ebrach, Germany, was used for an ice hockey championship with the inmates.

2 | **RAUMLABORBERLIN**
SILVER PEARL CONFERENCE CENTER AND SPA
Rostock, Germany

'Silver Pearl Congress Centre and Spa' was a temporary hotel and festival centre for 'Art goes Heiligendamm'. In appearance it alluded to the profile of the Hotel Kempinski, Heiligendamm, 'The White Pearl', where the 2007 G8 summit took place. It had a spa, a sauna, a golf course, comfortable suites with an ocean view, and a security fence. There, visitors could do what was prohibited in Heiligendamm: voice their opinion, demonstrate at the fence, and relax.

page 217
GRAHAM HUDSON
RESIDENCE
London, UK

For this project, Graham Hudson has taken up residence on the parade ground of Chelsea College of Art and Design's Millbank campus supported by the Henry Moore Foundation. As is typical of the artist's usual enthusiasm and grandiose tendencies, Hudson has embraced the residency by building and opening his studio for all to see on one of London's most visible plots.

THOMAS BRATZKE
Jazzstylecorner
CITY OF NAMES II
Berlin, Germany

Developed by Thomas Bratzke and organised in collaboration with Jazzstylecorner, Backjumps – The Live Issue #2, and Kunstraum Kreuzberg/Bethanien, a group of about 40 graffiti writers and street artists from Berlin and other cities around the world built a small city with the help of interested residents and kids from the Mariannenplatz neighbourhood in Kreuzberg, Berlin in the summer of 2005. The 'tag', the individual expression of the writer reduced to a signature, became the point of departure for the spatial structures and dwellings.

The graffiti writers, who usually take on foreign architecture in their creative outbursts, took on the roles of architects, landlords, and urban planners. Some of them even lived in their newly built homes; others left them to be used by the public. As a result, the City of Names – which stayed open to the public 24/7 – transformed its appearance daily.

Artists: Aris & Des, Jolie, Mizwa, Bus 126, Graff. Museum, KG, Poe, Mony, Try, Cream, Thief & Brom, Betty, Idee, Mr. Mucho, Babbo & Fiona, Nomad, Bosom & 2ndRound, CBS, Jost, Hesht, Nemo, Sear, Phos, Saint, Pegasus, Suzi, R.Schwarz, KHC, CAF, Akim, Point, Freaksgallery, Armsrock, El Cid, Angst, Hanna

1 | FRANZ HÖFNER, HARRY SACHS,
MICHAEL BOEHLER &
MARKUS LOHMANN
DOUANEVILLE
Hamburg, Germany

This was a temporary settlement
at the former customs building of
Hamburg's free-harbour.

2 | FRANZ HÖFNER & HARRY SACHS
ROSAPARK
Kunstverein Freiburg,
Freiburg, Germany

For Rosapark, the German artistic
duo converted an industrial storage
space into a city model, accessible
by a little train.

DADARA
CHECKPOINT DREAMYOURTOPIA
Black Rock Desert, Nevada, USA

Checkpoint Dreamyourtopia by Dutch artist Dadara is a border control checkpoint to enter one's own dreams. Operated by the Department of Dreamland Security, which will ensure a safe and smooth passage into your own dream world, it was built in the Nevada desert during the Burning Man Festival. Participants wishing to enter their dreams had to fill out immigration form WXRZYQ SFG 23587-492 A and go through immigration procedures and interrogation, after which they were granted permission to enter their dreams and received an accompanying passport to the Land of Dreams.

FRIENDS WITH YOU
RAINBOW VALLEY
Aventura Mall, Miami, Florida

This indoor playground by Friends With You tells the enchanting story of a miniature mountain that loses his family and goes on a search for other small mountains to play with. This adventure is filled with rainbow blasts, magic, and heart-moving moments.

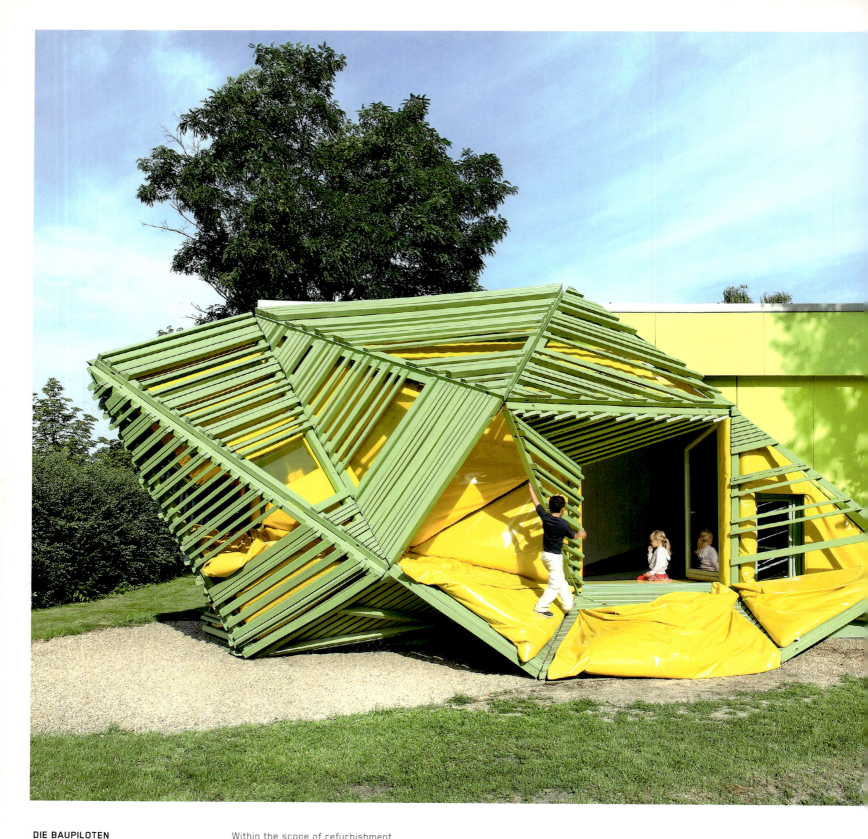

DIE BAUPILOTEN
KINDERGARTEN TAKA–TUKA–LAND
Berlin, Germany

Within the scope of refurbishment, the Baupiloten created an entirely newly conceived world from the temporary structure of the kindergarten as imagined by the children who attended it. The results are interactive and communicative interior spaces, as well as a multifunctional façade according to Astrid Lindgren's story. The construction costs were extremely low due to the use of recycling material and the economical renewal of the damaged building stock.

RICHARD WOODS
1 | **FLORA & FAUNA**
Milton Keynes Gallery, UK

Richard Woods's installations are formal displays that take over the entire space, from floor to the wall. The juxtaposition of eccentric shapes and colours achieves a sense of saturation within space, with a dense and dramatic effect.

RICHARD WOODS
2 | **INNOVATION–INVESTMENT–PROGRESS**
Liverpool Biennial, UK

CLAUS RICHTER &
TOBIAS REHBERGER
SHOWTIME

The Design Annual,
Frankfurt / Main, Germany

Commissioned by the Frankfurt-
based agency Stylepark, the two
artists Claus Richter and Tobias
Rehberger designed the interior of
the trade fair The Design Annual
2008. The theme of the exhibition and events programme was
'showtime' and the artists created
a psychedelic environment featuring
flying pies, weeping trees, confused
giraffes, speaking clocks, and owls
that play the flute.

HELEN & HARD
THE GEOPARK
Kjerringholmen, Stavanger, Norway

One of the most urgent challenges facing the Norwegian oil industry is the future recycling of its material and knowledge-related assets. The Geopark is part of the official programme for celebrating the Stavanger region as a European Capital of Culture in 2008. Its theme is the relationship between the unique material and knowledge base of the local petroleum industry and its transfer value to architecture and urban development. In cooperation with the Norwegian Petroleum Museum, partners in the industry and local youth groups, the project has been developed as an experimental urban space. Surfaces and installations are constructed out of recycled and reshaped elements from the petroleum sector taken from abandoned fields, offshore bases, equipment suppliers, and scrap heaps.

**ANNA GALTAROSSA &
DANIEL GONZÁLEZ
HOMELESS ROCKET WITH
CHANDELIERS**
Milano, Italy

Homeless Rocket With Chandeliers is the transformation of a fully operational thirty-metre construction crane into a rocket-city with chandeliers. This building machine has been elevated to the status of art by being contaminated with objects and materials that refer to street culture and the freedom that it can transmit. Construction workers use the crane daily, and it will remain in via Massimiano (Lambrate, Milan) until redevelopment work in another area of the neighbourhood has been completed.

JAVIER SENOSIAIN
NAUTILUS HOUSE
Naucalpan, Mexico

The Nautilus House by Mexican architect Javier Senosiain was built in the form of a big snail whose structure works as an evocative shell: resistance, protection, and shelter. It is a continuous, large, integral area with liberating shapes and changing lights that follow the natural rhythm of man's movements.

LIZA LOU
TRAILOR, KITCHEN

Liza Lou is an artist whose work combines visionary, conceptual, traditional, and vernacular approaches to create a new kind of sculptural experience. She is best known for her ambitious sculptural installations, each of which were years in the making. The luminous patterned surfaces of her sculptural environments are like walk-in paintings.

FASHION ARCHITECTURE TASTE (FAT)
KESSELSKRAMER
Amsterdam, Netherlands

This project transforms an unused church interior in Amsterdam into the offices of an advertising agency. A number of objects at different scales were chosen from a series of sketches faxed to the client. These were placed within the church to provide workstations, platforms, chill-out areas, a library, and a TV room. The objects chosen – a wooden fort, a fragment of a shed, and a life guards' watch tower – are subject to distortions in scale, fragmentation, and juxtaposition, reinforcing their strangeness within the context of the church. These major elements are supplemented by a number of smaller ones, which include fragments of a football pitch, picnic tables, hedges, and fences, as well as a number of pieces of furniture, ornaments, and objects bought by the client from flea markets.

page 231 / 1
FASHION ARCHITECTURE TASTE (FAT)
YOU MAKE ME FEEL
Northumberland, UK

This summer house, built originally for English Heritage at Belsay Hall, Northumberland, now resides at Grizedale Forest in the Lake District. The design is based on a Romanesque church. It is clad in thousands of metal discs, which create a pixelated pattern depicting oversized Romanesque decoration.

page 231 / 2
NATHAN COLEY
CAMOUFLAGE CHURCH
Santiago de Compostella, Spain

The Camouflage Church, painted in stripes, was installed in the famous pilgrimage destination Santiago de Compostella by artist Nathan Coley.

CHAPTER 06

BLOW UP

ROBBIE ROWLANDS

RACHEL WHITEREAD

The verb 'to blow up' indicates a variety of practices in English: it describes the act of pumping or filling something up; the act of deliberate explosion or detonation; or the use of magnification and exaggeration – that is, blowing something out of proportion. Tongue-in-cheek, this chapter covers all three levels of meaning, bridging the gap between spatially expanding structures and shuttered and ruptured constructions, all of which are blown out of proportion.

Maintaining the accelerated pace of the previous chapters, this final and concluding section culminates in a firework of seemingly paradox architectural and artistic ventures that magnify the abandonment of customary approaches to built space. The projects range from inflatable structures by Interaction Design Lab, Airscape, or Mass Studies to tents and marquees by Tracey Emin and Studio Orta. Many of the projects seek to break up or even annul space as we know it. Take, for example, the soft, bird-nest-like loungescape called The Third Room, built from 1.5 million cable links by students at the Academy of Fine Arts Munich, or Tokujin Yoshioka's poetic recreations of seemingly formless and fluid entities. However, it is British Artist Richard Wilson, with his 2007 site-specific installation Turning the Place Over, who offers the most ingenious extrapolation of Gordon Matta-Clark's artistic heritage. For this project, Wilson cut an eight-metre-wide circular section from the façade of an abandoned building and attached it to a giant rotator, allowing it to oscillate in three dimensions.

However disparate and diverse the projects in this chapter may seem, they all share a visionary approach to creating intense sensory experiences of space, leaving spectators wondering what they are witnessing.

MICHAEL ELMGREEN & INGAR DRAGSET

This open-air pavilion is used as a stage during the festival season in the summer, and as an attraction for excursionists and flaneurs. With great ease, the pavilion integrates itself into the landscape and, through its topographical configuration, reinterprets formal elements of the surrounding landscape garden – playing with perspective and visual relations, with contraction and expansion, with enclosure and opening.

The staging of views and spatial sequences, the framing and hiding of points of attraction, often achieved by the meandering layout of paths in the traditional landscape garden, is a theme taken up by varying the elevation of the incision to achieve the effects. The stage roof is designed as an autonomous, sculptured object. Suspended above the landscape at the level of the tree canopies, it is placed among the groups of trees as if it were one of them. The shiny metal surface on the outside reflects the sky and the trees, turning the structure into a cloud tower.

page 236
OLAFUR ELIASSON
THE BLIND PAVILION
Videy Island, Iceland

First situated on the roof of the
Danish Pavilion at the 50th Venice
Biennale in Italy in 2003, the blind
pavilion was later exhibited on a
hilltop on Videy Island in Iceland.
This pavilion is a double-layer steel
structure, glazed with angular panes
of clear and translucent black glass.
Visitors can walk between the layers
of glass, which partially obscure and
partially reflect the surroundings.

SIMPARCH
CLEAN LIVIN'
Wendover, Utah

With Clean Livin', a solar-powered,
refurbished military Quonset hut and
surrounding grounds, SIMPARCH
explores the unique conditions and
paradoxes presented by the striking,
contested landscape of Wendover,
a high-desert town and former army
airfield that straddles the border
between Utah and Nevada.

In sharp contrast to the original
use of the base, Clean Livin' is a
metabolic proving ground, where
conscious use of resources and
the body's own metabolic energy
alter the normal expectations of
daily living. Besides providing basic
habitation, a primary goal of Clean
Livin' is to recover and transform all
materials brought to the site.

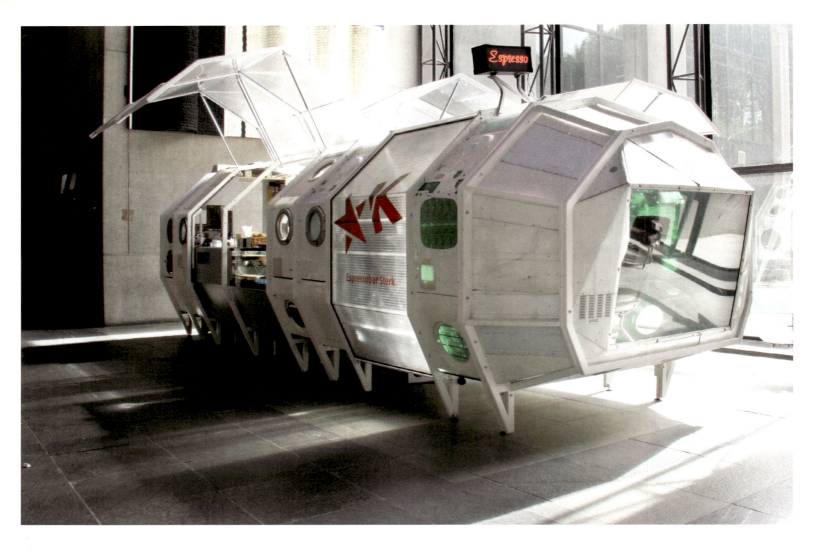

2012 ARCHITECTEN
SPACE STATION
Rotterdam, Netherlands

The partners of 2012 Architecten, an
architecture firm in the Netherlands,
incorporates in their design approach
materials that would otherwise be
thrown away. 2012 Architecten constructed this pavilion out of discarded
washing machines.

BUREAU DES MÉSARCHITECTURES
Didier Fiuza Faustino
H-BOX

The H-Box is a mobile space to display
video art for Hermès International.
The pavilion is composed of modules
of highly resistant lightweight materials, easily assembled, disassembled,
and transported for travel around
the world.

TOM SACHS
LUNAR MODULE
Gagosian Gallery, New York, USA

The huge, intricately built lunar module that is the centrepiece of Tom Sachs's 'SPACE PROGRAM' exhibition at the Gagosian Gallery features a fully stocked booze cabinet, toolkit, and soundtrack necessary for survival on an alien planet. Using his prodigious technical skills to expound on the make-do ethics of bricolage, Sachs refashions the world out of simple stuff – foam-core, hot-glue, and standard materials, scavenged or readily available from do-it-yourself catalogues.

ANDY HOLDEN
THE THIRD ATTEMPT
Vijfhuizen, Netherlands

This is the third in a series of temporary outdoor 'boulder' works, presented as an interruption in the landscape. It is sculpture as an event or encounter, a temporary intervention on a monumental scale, which gives it a peculiar relationship to public sculpture and the flat landscape of the Dutch polder.

TOBIAS REHBERGER
THE WORLD NEXT DOOR TO OUTSIDE

German artist Tobias Rehberger
works in the wider sphere of design and architecture, thriving on
chance connections and unexpected
encounters.

SABINE GROSS
BLACK SCREAM
Neuer Berliner Kunstverein,
Berlin, Germany

1 | **MICHAEL ELMGREEN &
INGAR DRAGSET**
**ELEVATED GALLERY / POWERLESS
STRUCTURES, FIG. 146**

2 | **KREISSL KERBER**
COLLAPSED TV-TOWER
Kunstmuseum, Zwickau, Germany

Kreissl Kerber are attracted by the
places where a town's system of order
breaks down, as these are free of
narrow-minded planning regulations
and thus open to uncommon architectural ideas and individual solutions.

STUDIO ORTA
Lucy & Jorge Orta
1 | **ANTARCTICA**
Hangar Bicocca, Milan, Italy

The 'Antarctica' exhibition in
the Hangar Bicocca, curated by
Bartolomeo Pietromarchi, represents
the first complete public showing of
the works created by the artists
as a result of their expedition to
the frozen continent. Among many
other pieces, the emblematic dome
architectures are exhibited. These
made up the village that was actually
installed in Antarctica.

STUDIO ORTA
Lucy & Jorge Orta
2 | **ANTARCTIC VILLAGE / NO BORDERS,
EPHEMERAL INSTALLATION IN
ANTARCTICA**

In early 2007, the artists installed
'Antarctic Village' in Antarctica.
Taking place during the Austral summer, the ephemeral installation co-
incided with the last of the scientific
expeditions before the winter months,
when the ice mass becomes too thick
to traverse. The work consisted of
fifty dome dwellings, hand-stitched
with nation flags, fragments of cloth-
ing, webbing, and silkscreen print by
Lucy Orta, Professor of Art, Fashion,
and the Environment at the University
of the Arts, London.

TRACEY EMIN
EVERYONE I HAVE EVER SLEPT WITH
1963–1995
London, UK

Tracey Emin's Everyone I Have Ever
Slept With 1963–1995 tent embroi-
dered with the names of those the
title suggests, featuring more than
100 names.

1 | DANA AND KARLA KARWAS
PARTY DRESS
Various locations

Party dress began as an idea about taking the relationship between architecture and fashion to the next level. The dress uses performance as a vessel to blend the drama and accelerated pace of fashion with the scale and processes of architecture. Party Dress has the ability to adapt to each environment dynamically, creating a unique and provocative experience.

2 | ID-LAB
C.I.C.C.I.O.
Triennale di Milano, Italy

CICCIO or the Curiously Inflated Computer Controlled Interactive Object is a light, inflatable, transportable space made from sewn pieces of nylon.

page 245
NABA DESIGN SCHOOL
NABABOOM: DESIGN PARASSITA
NABA campus, Milan, Italy

A network of illuminated camping tents installed on the NABA campus in Milan, each of which becomes an original micro-exhibition space containing the works of the students.

FRIENDS WITH YOU
DREAM MAKER

Indianapolis Museum of Art, USA

This installation is on display in the
lobby of the IMA Indianapolis Museum
of Art. The giant sculpture functions
as a miniature solar system that
pertains directly to one's luck and
dreams. As the mobile rotates on its
axis, your luck and the possibilities
are constantly changing.

YAYOI KUSAMA
DOTS OBSESSION
Le Consortium, Dijon, France
Les Abattoirs, Toulouse, France
The Kennedy Center,
Washington D.C., USA

As the title suggests, these works by
Japanese artist Yayoi Kusama share
an obsession with repetition, pattern,
and accumulation.

TOPOTEK 1
PNEUMATIC
Wolfsburg, Germany

For the Landesgartenschau
Wolfsburg, twenty-four inflatable objects and fifteen cubes made of foam
rubber coloured pink and baby-pink
are strewn across the lawn. Wheeled
wagons, rings, air-filled wands, balls
in various dimensions, and two large,
exuberantly-coloured bouncy mats
catch people's attention and attract
anyone wishing to play on the meadow
next to the horse paddock.

page 249
RYUMEI FUJIKI + FUJIKI STUDIO, KOU::ARC
AQUA-SCAPE
Tokamachi, Niigata, Japan

This floating object was developed
by Ryumei Fujiki in cooperation with
students as a prototype of flowing,
lightweight mobile architecture.
It combines origami, the ancient
Japanese craft, with state-of-the-
art materials. Plastic sheets with a
net structure of intertwined polyeth-
ylene fibres and sine-curve creases
were folded and woven crosswise
into a three-dimensional object.

1 | **RACHEL WHITEREAD**
WATER TOWER
New York, USA

This physically present and yet ephemeral public sculpture by Rachel Whiteread is a translucent resin cast of the interior of a wooden water tank that was raised seven stories to rest upon the steel tower frame of a SoHo rooftop.

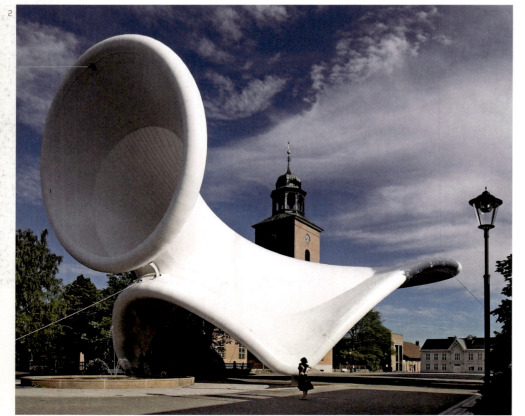

pages 250/2, 251
SNØHETTA
TUBALOON
Kongsberg Jazz Festival, Norway

The Tubaloon is a membrane structure designed by the Norwegian architecture firm Snøhetta to serve as the main stage at Scandinavia's reputable Kongsberg Jazz Festival. The mounting of Tubaloon will recur annually and stand for three weeks' time before the structure is stored in standard containers for the rest of the year. Acoustically, the Tubaloon is a dynamic and tuneable venue. The form provides a classic clamshell-like shape over the audience to keep quiet performances intimate while the PVC fabric construction is nearly transparent to sound during amplified performances.

SNØHETTA
TUBALOON
Kongsberg Jazz Festival, Norway

Air Forest is a temporary public pavilion installed in City Park, Denver in Colorado, USA, for Dialog:City, an arts and cultural event during the 2008 Democratic National Convention. Air Forest is a pneumatic structure composed of hexagonal canopy units that are interconnected as one large piece of fabric, which are then inflated from blowers that are located at the base inside its columns.

The Berlin-based studio AIRSCAPE creates amorphous and mobile architectural spaces. The lightweight all-purpose inflatable tents are suitable for any kind of event or presentation – indoor and outdoor – and can be erected within minutes.

BORIS BERNASKONI
SPACE FOR DISCOVERY
Moscow, Russia

**LAVA / LABORATORY FOR VISONARY
ARCHITECTURE ASIA PACIFIC**
Chris Bosse
ENTRY PARADISE
Zeche Zollverein, Essen, Germany

Microscopic cell structures served
as the inspiration for the design of a
pavilion that is reminiscent of irregu-
lar natural forms like foam, sponge,
or coral reefs. The phenomenology
and structure of microorganisms
such as coral polyps or radiolarians
are the basis of the computer simu-
lation of naturally evolving systems.

page 256
CHRIS BOSSE
with students st the University of Technology, Sydney
DIGITAL ORIGAMI
Sydney, Australia

This arrangement of 3500 recycled cardboard molecules in different abstract shapes and illuminated with neon light is the work of the students at the University of Technology in Sydney and architect Chris Bosse. The digital origami exhibition is a progressive display of reinventing ancient traditions in digital parameters. The modules of two different designs have been laser-cut, stacked, and installed to produce an innovative installation that almost entirely fills a gallery across several floors.

page 257 / 1
PROJECT OR
Ran Ankory, Francesco Brenta, Maya Carni, Christoph Klemmt, Laura Micalizzi, and Elisa Oddone
OR
Milan, Italy

OR is a vortex-shaped surface that reacts to sunlight. The polygonal segments of the surface react to ultraviolet light, mapping the position and intensity of solar rays. When in the shade, the segments of OR are translucent white. However, when hit by sunlight, they become coloured, flooding the space below with a variety of hues.

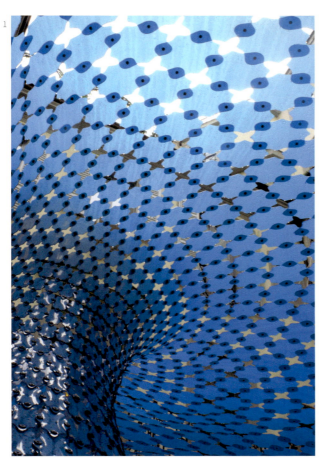

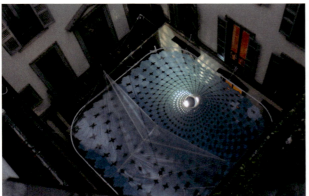

2 | **BALL NOGUES STUDIO**
MAXIMILIAN'S SCHELL
Los Angeles, CA, USA

This architectural installation is partly a twenty-first century tensile structure and partly a tribute to Disney Studio's sci-fi cult film 'The Black Hole'. The installation is designed to warp the flow of an outdoor space with a feather-weight rendition of 'the deadliest force in the universe' constructed in tinted mylar-like stained glass. It swirls above the outdoor courtyard all summer long. An assembly of 512 unique instances of a single but parametrically variable component, the canopy's extreme intricacy and repetitiveness pay homage to actor Maximilian Schell's character, Dr. Reinhardt, in 'The Black Hole', a tyrant who wishes to harness the 'power of the vortex' and possess the great truth of the unknown!

NOX
Lars Spuybroek
SON-O-HOUSE
Son en Breugel, Netherlands

Located in a large industrial park, the Son-O-House is a public pavilion. The structure is both an architectural and a sound installation that allows people not just to hear sound in a musical structure, but also to participate in its composition. It is an instrument, score, and studio at the same time. A sound work, made by composer Edwin van der Heide, is continuously generating new aural patterns activated by sensors picking up the movements of visitors.

page 259
MASS STUDIES
RING DOME
Milan, Italy

Ring Dome Milan is the second in a series of Ring Domes constructed around the world, starting from New York. In collaboration with Storefront for Art and Architecture Gallery and design magazine 'Abitare', Ring Dome Milan was built at the intersection inside Galleria Vittorio Emanuele for the Furniture Fair. The Ring Dome is a dome-shaped structure composed of about 1000 plastic hula hoops.

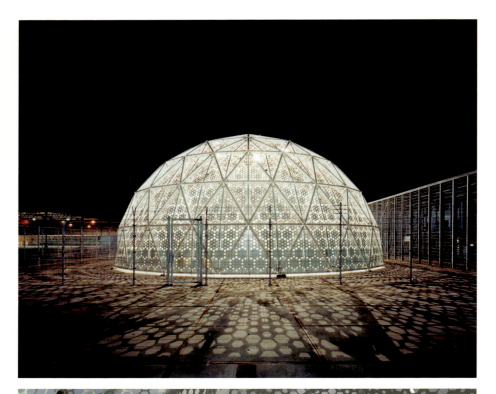

CUSTOMR
Willem van der Sluis
SPORT DOMES
Zaandam, Netherlands

Catering to almost 600 prisoners, the Zaandam prison north of Amsterdam is a floating structure consisting of two boats docked in the harbour. Two three-storey-high steel domes stand ashore next to boats. In response to a government commission that called for more sports in Dutch prisons, the domes were designed by Willem van der Sluis of Customr, an Amsterdam industrial design studio. The two domes have perforated shells that let in sun, wind, and rain and form an intricate, security-conscious pattern that is dense at the bottom and looser higher up. Inmates can look out without being seen.

page 261 / 1
ECOLOGICSTUDIO
Claudia Pasquero and Marco Poletto
STEMCLOUD V2.0
Seville Biennale of Art and
Architecture, Spain

The STEMcloud v2.0 project proposes the development and testing of an architectural prototype operating as an oxygen-producing machine. Its technological matrix will operate as a breeding ground for micro-ecologies found in the local river of Seville, the Guadalquivir, and will involve the public in the breeding process. Visitors will be transformed into ecologists, the STEM blocks into microhabitats, and the gallery into an oxygenating garden or, perhaps, a laboratory.

page 261 / 2
ECOLOGICSTUDIO
FIBROUS ROOM
Garanti Gallery, Istanbul, Turkey

Fibrous Room, an installation by ecoLogicStudio with Tusba (Garanti Gallery, Istanbul), is an investigation into the emergent properties of complex fibre-reinforced, cement-based structures. The material prototype constructed in Garanti Galleri is an assemblage defined through a three-dimensional extrusion of a pattern grid found in Islamic art by means of a 'weaving operator'. Here, concrete has escaped the trap of rigid form to come back to life.

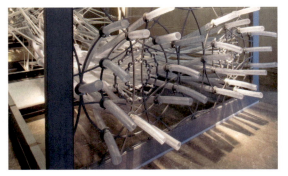

ACADEMY OF FINE ARTS MUNICH / INTERIOR DESIGN
THE THIRD ROOM
Munich, Germany

Under the direction of their professors Maria Auböck, Carmen and Urs Greutmann, and Peter Sapp, fifty-two students of interior design developed and built an installation entitled The Third Room made of 1.5 million cable links. Cable links are usually associated with all kinds of montages on site – with cables above ground and below, dealing with information and energy transport. This installation offers a sensuous experience in a nonverbal way, employing a commonly-used architectonic material.

TOKUJIN YOSHIOKA

1 | **SUPER FIBER REVOLUTION**

Axis Gallery, Tokyo, Japan

Tokujin's approach towards structures of the future follows the idea that, to achieve great strength, small, light fibres should be systematically organised.

TOKUJIN YOSHIOKA

2 | **TORNADO**

Design Miami, USA

As 'Designer of the Year 2007', Tokujin created a large space installation entitled Tornado by using two million transparent straws. As a cloud and snow, thousands and millions of the particles add up to a white structure. By simply using transparent straws, he created a natural phenomenon: a tornado inside the room.

PEZO VON ELLRICHSHAUSEN
FORESTAL
Santiago de Chile, Chile

This forest-like installation by Mauricio
· Pezo and Sofía von Ellrichshausen
consists of fifty-five columns made
from crumpled pieces of paper.

1 | **TILMAN WENDLAND**
UNTITLED
Ideal City – 'Invisible Cities' Exhibition,
Potsdam, Germany

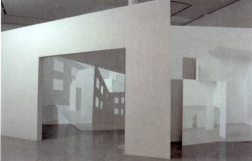

page 266 / 2
ERIK OLOFSEN
STATE OF DELUSION
Bilbao Arte – Bilbao, Spain and
P/////AKT – Amsterdam,
Netherlands

The works of Erik Olofsen manipu-
late the physical space that houses
them with false walls and wood, but
often also with video projections and
other perceptual means. The optical
illusions, the distorted images, the
play of light and shadow generated
by the projectors make crossing the
exhibition hall a new sensory, almost
dizzying, experience.

page 267
ERIK OLOFSEN
MENTAL POLLUTION
Bilbao Arte – Bilbao, Spain

ROBBIE ROWLANDS
THE UPHOLSTERER
Grendas Bus Depot – Dandenong,
Victoria, Australia

The Upholsterer was a site-specific installation shown at Grendas
Decomissioned Bus Depot prior to
its demolition. The work was set in
the old upholstery workshop situated in a house from the 1950s.

RICHARD WILSON
TURNING THE PLACE OVER
Liverpool, UK

The work Turning the Place Over
consists of a vast eight-metre-diam-
eter ovoid section from the façade
of a currently disused building in
Liverpool. The section was mounted
on a central spindle, allowing it to
rotate. As it does so, the façade not
only becomes completely inverted
but also oscillates into the building
and out into the street, revealing the
interior of the structure. It is flush
with the building at only one point
during its rotation.

MICHAEL ELMGREEN &
INGAR DRAGSET
TAKING PLACE
Kunsthalle Zürich, Switzerland

ERIK GÖNGRICH
SILENT RESIDENCY
Theater der Welt,
Flughafen Leipzig / Halle, Germany

This installation by Berlin-based artist
Erik Göngrich was created for the
duration of AusFlugHafenSicht as part
of the International Festival Theater
der Welt in Halle / Leipzig, Germany.

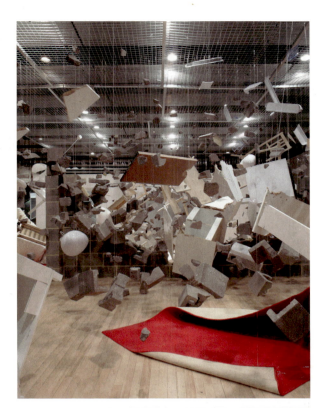

LOS CARPINTEROS
SHOW ROOM

The Hayward Gallery, London, UK

Installation of a smashed-up apartment by Cuban art group Los Carpinteros for the 'Psycho Buildings' exhibition at the Hayward Gallery.

INDEX

INDEX

SPACECRAFT 2
<u>MORE FLEETING ARCHITECTURE AND HIDEOUTS</u>

Edited by Robert Klanten and Lukas Feireiss
All texts written by Lukas Feireiss

Layout by Birga Meyer for Gestalten
Divider page layout based upon designs
by Daniel Adolph & Mario Lombardo
Cover Photography by Lukas Schaller
Art Direction by Robert Klanten
Typeface: Blender by Nik Thoenen
Foundry: www.gestalten.com/fonts

Project Management by Julian Sorge for Gestalten
Production Management by Martin Bretschneider for Gestalten
Copy-editing by Kitty Bolhöfer
Proofreading by Matthew Gaskins
Printed by Offsetdruckerei Grammlich GmbH, Pliezhausen, Germany

Published by Gestalten, Berlin 2009
ISBN 978-3-89955-233-1

For more information, please check www.gestalten.com

Bibliographic information published by the Deutsche Nationalbibliothek.
The Deutsche Nationalbibliothek lists this publication in the Deutsche
Nationalbibliografie; detailed bibliographic data are available on the
internet at http://dnb.d-nb.de.

None of the content in this book was published in exchange for pay-
ment by commercial parties or designers; Gestalten selected all
included work based solely on its artistic merit.

This book was printed according to the internationally accepted FSC
standards for environmental protection, which specify requirements
for an environmental management system.

Mixed Sources
Product group from well-managed
forests and other controlled sources
www.fsc.org Cert no. IMO-COC-028001
© 1996 Forest Stewardship Council

Gestalten is a climate neutral company and so are our products. We
collaborate with the non-profit carbon offset provider myclimate
(www.myclimate.org) to neutralize the company's carbon footprint
produced through our worldwide business activities by investing in
projects that reduce CO_2 emissions (www.gestalten.com/myclimate).

Protect our planet

SEAN GODSELL ARCHITECTS

DO-HO SUH

TOKUJIN YOSHIOKA

ANDY HOLDEN